Cambridge Elements ≡

Elements in the Philosophy of Martin Heidegger
edited by
Filippo Casati
Lehigh University
Daniel O. Dahlstrom
Boston University

HEIDEGGER'S CONCEPT OF SCIENCE

Paul Goldberg
St. John's College

CAMBRIDGE
UNIVERSITY PRESS

CAMBRIDGE
UNIVERSITY PRESS

Shaftesbury Road, Cambridge CB2 8EA, United Kingdom

One Liberty Plaza, 20th Floor, New York, NY 10006, USA

477 Williamstown Road, Port Melbourne, VIC 3207, Australia

314–321, 3rd Floor, Plot 3, Splendor Forum, Jasola District Centre,
New Delhi – 110025, India

103 Penang Road, #05–06/07, Visioncrest Commercial, Singapore 238467

Cambridge University Press is part of Cambridge University Press & Assessment,
a department of the University of Cambridge.

We share the University's mission to contribute to society through the pursuit of
education, learning and research at the highest international levels of excellence.

www.cambridge.org
Information on this title: www.cambridge.org/9781009523554

DOI: 10.1017/9781009523523

When citing this work, please include a reference to the DOI 10.1017/9781009523523

First published 2024

A catalogue record for this publication is available from the British Library

ISBN 978-1-009-52355-4 Hardback
ISBN 978-1-009-52353-0 Paperback
ISSN 2976-5668 (online)
ISSN 2976-565X (print)

Cambridge University Press & Assessment has no responsibility for the persistence or
accuracy of URLs for external or third-party internet websites referred to in this
publication and does not guarantee that any content on such websites is, or will
remain, accurate or appropriate.

Heidegger's Concept of Science

Elements in the Philosophy of Martin Heidegger

DOI: 10.1017/9781009523523
First published online: November 2024

Paul Goldberg
St. John's College

Author for correspondence: Paul Goldberg, paul.goldberg92@gmail.com

Abstract: This Element argues that Heidegger's concept of science has two core features. Heidegger critiques a *security-oriented concept of science*, which he associates with the dominance of physics in modern science and metaphysics and with a progressive resistance among philosophers and scientists to ontological questioning. Meanwhile, Heidegger advances an *access-oriented concept of science*, on which science is essentially founded on ontological disclosures but also constantly open to the possibility of new revolutionary disclosures. This Element discusses how these commitments develop in Heidegger's early and later thinking, and argues that they inform his views on the history of Western metaphysics and on the possibilities for human flourishing that modernity, and modern science specifically, affords. The Element also discusses Heidegger's dialogue with Werner Heisenberg about quantum physics; and throughout, it highlights points of contact and divergence between Heidegger and other philosophers of science such as Karl Popper, Thomas Kuhn, Paul Feyerabend, and Helen Longino.

Keywords: Martin Heidegger, science, physicalism, technology, Werner Heisenberg

ISBNs: 9781009523554 (HB), 9781009523530 (PB), 9781009523523 (OC)
ISSNs: 2976-5668 (online), 2976-565X (print)

Contents

Science is not an occupation, not a business, not a diversion, but is rather the *possibility of the existence of human beings*, and not something into which one happens by chance.

BCAP 5

[S]cience should never be equated with its results, results that are then passed from hand to hand....[W]hat is essential to science does not lie in what can merely be handed down, passed along from hand to hand, but rather in that which is appropriated ever anew.

GA27 32

Texts and Method of Citation

References to Heidegger's writing are given using the following abbreviations followed by page numbers – e.g., "*BCAP* 5" refers to page 5 of *Basic Concepts of Aristotelian Philosophy*.

BCAP   *Basic Concepts of Aristotelian Philosophy*. Trans. Robert D. Metcalf and Mark B. Tanzer. (Bloomington: Indiana University Press, 2009).

BFL   *Bremen and Freiburg Lectures: Insight into That Which Is and Basic Principles of Thinking*. Trans. Andrew Mitchell. (Bloomington: Indiana University Press, 2012).

BH   *Becoming Heidegger: On the Trail of His Early Occasional Writings, 1910–1927*. Ed. Theodore Kisiel and Thomas Sheehan. (Evanston, IL: Northwestern University Press, 2007).

BPP   *The Basic Problems of Phenomenology*. Trans. Albert Hofstadter. (Bloomington: Indiana University Press, 1982). Revised edition.

BPWS   *Basic Problems of Phenomenology: Winter Semester 1919/1920*. Trans. Scott M. Campbell. (New York: Bloomsbury, 2013).

CP   *Contributions to Philosophy (of the Event)*. Trans. Richard Rojcewicz and Daniela Vallega-Neu. (Bloomington: Indiana University Press, 2012).

CT   *The Concept of Time: The First Draft of* Being and Time. Trans. Ingo Farin. (New York: Bloomsbury, 2011).

EN   *European Nihilism*. In *Nietzsche: Volume IV: Nihilism*, pp. 1–196. Trans. Frank A. Capuzzi. Ed. David Farrell Krell. (San Francisco, CA: Harper & Row, 1982).

EP   *The End of Philosophy*. Trans. and ed. Joan Stambaugh. (New York: Harper & Row, 1973).

ET   *The Essence of Truth: On Plato's Cave Allegory and* Theaetetus. Trans. Ted Sadler. (London: Continuum, 2002).

GA7   *Vorträge und Aufsätze. Gesamtausgabe*, Volume 7. Ed. Friedrich-Wilhelm von Herrmann. (Frankfurt am Main: Vittorio Klostermann, 2000).

GA23   *Geschichte der Philosophie von Thomas Aquin bis Kant. Gesamtausgabe*, Volume 23. Ed. Friedrich-Wilhelm von Herrmann. (Frankfurt am Main: Vittorio Klostermann, 2006).

GA27   *Einleitung in die Philosophie. Gesamtausgabe*, Volume 27. Ed. Friedrich-Wilhelm von Herrmann. (Frankfurt am Main: Vittorio Klostermann, 1996).

GA76   *Leitgedanken zur Entstehung der Metaphysik, der neuzeitlichen Wissenschaft und der modernen Technik.* Gesamtausgabe, Volume 76. Ed. Friedrich-Wilhelm von Herrmann. (Frankfurt am Main: Vittorio Klostermann, 2009).

GA90   *Zu Ernst Jünger. Gesamtausgabe,* Volume 90. Ed. Friedrich-Wilhelm von Herrmann. (Frankfurt am Main: Vittorio Klostermann, 2004).

HCCR   *The Heidegger Controversy: A Critical Reader.* Ed. Richard Wolin. (Cambridge, MA: MIT Press, 1993).

HCT   *History of the Concept of Time: Prolegomena.* Trans. Theodore Kisiel. (Bloomington: Indiana University Press, 1985).

IM   *Introduction to Metaphysics.* Trans. Gregory Fried and Richard Polt. (New Haven, CT: Yale University Press, 2014). Second edition.

IPR   *Introduction to Phenomenological Research.* Trans. Daniel O. Dahlstrom. (Bloomington: Indiana University Press, 2005).

LQT   *Logic: The Question of Truth.* Trans. Thomas Sheehan. (Bloomington: Indiana University Press, 2010).

LT   *Four Seminars: Le Thor 1967, 1968, 1969, Zähringen 1973.* Trans. Andrew Mitchell and François Raffoul. (Bloomington: Indiana University Press, 2003).

NDHB   "Nihilism as Determined by the History of Being." In *Nietzsche: Volume IV: Nihilism*, pp. 197–250. Trans. Frank A. Capuzzi. Ed. David Farrell Krell. (San Francisco, CA: Harper & Row, 1982).

OBT   *Off the Beaten Track.* Ed. and trans. Julian Young and Kenneth Haynes. (Cambridge: Cambridge University Press, 2002).

OHF   *Ontology – The Hermeneutics of Facticity.* Trans. John van Buren. (Bloomington: Indiana University Press, 1999).

P   *Pathmarks.* Ed. William McNeill. (Cambridge: Cambridge University Press, 1998).

PIA   *Phenomenological Interpretations of Aristotle: Initiation into Phenomenological Research.* Trans. Richard Rojcewicz. (Bloomington: Indiana University Press, 2001).

PIE   *Phenomenology of Intuition and Expression.* Trans. Tracy Colony. (London: Continuum, 2010).

PR   *The Principle of Reason.* Trans. Reginald Lilly. (Bloomington: Indiana University Press, 1991).

PS   *Plato's Sophist.* Trans. Richard Rojcewicz and André Schuwer. (Bloomington: Indiana University Press, 2003).

QCT "The Question Concerning Technology." In *The Question Concerning Technology and Other Essays*, pp. 3–35. Trans. and ed. William Lovitt. (New York: Garland, 1977).

QT *The Question Concerning the Thing: On Kant's Doctrine of the Transcendental Principles*. Trans. James D. Reid and Benjamin D. Crowe. (New York: Rowman and Littlefield International, 2018).

SR "Science and Reflection." In *The Question Concerning Technology and Other Essays*, pp. 155–82. Trans. and ed. William Lovitt. (New York: Garland, 1977).

SZ *Sein und Zeit*. (Tübingen: Max Niemeyer Verlag, 2006). English translation: *Being and Time*. Trans. John Macquarrie and Edward Robinson. (New York: Harper & Row, 1962).

TB *On Time and Being*. Trans. Joan Stambaugh. (New York: Harper & Row, 1972).

TDP *Towards the Definition of Philosophy*. Trans. Ted Sadler. (London: Continuum, 2008).

WCT *What Is Called Thinking?* Trans. J. Glenn Gray. (New York: Perennial, 1976).

Z *Zollikon Seminars: Protocols – Conversations – Letters*. Trans. Franz Mayr and Richard Askay. Ed. Medard Boss. (Evanston, IL: Northwestern University Press, 2001).

1 Introduction: Heidegger's Concept of Science

This essay is structured around a core argument. Throughout his career, Martin Heidegger criticizes the view that science's primary aim is to develop increasingly comprehensive and successful theories (taken in a broad sense) – i.e., the view that science primarily seeks to identify sets of propositions or develop models capable of explaining and predicting an ever-wider range of empirical phenomena, with the implicit aim of developing a final, complete (and, thus, maximally secure) theory. Call this the *security-oriented concept of science* (SCS). In its stead, Heidegger advances an alternative concept of science; he believes science's primary aim is to open up access to some unseen, unappreciated, or forgotten piece of reality,[1] and that such access is achieved, above all, by ontological disclosures; call this the *access-oriented concept of science* (ACS). The distinction between SCS and ACS might seem vague, and my task below is

---

[1] NB: throughout this work, "reality" is used in a broad sense to refer in an ontologically neutral way to individual entities and kinds of entities. This usage is distinct from the technical senses in which Heidegger sometimes uses *Realität* (to refer to the realm of the purely present-at-hand – see, e.g., *SZ* 211) or *Wirklichkeit* (to refer to a metaphysics of "objecthood" – see, e.g., SR 157–63). On the latter, see Section 5.1.

to clarify it. But the key point to bear in mind is that Heidegger thinks that access to reality must be reestablished ever anew via revolutionary ontological disclosures, and indeed, that science's epistemic virtue lies in scientists' willingness to surrender (rather than secure) their most cherished theories and concepts in order achieve this access.

I argue that in both mature phases of his career – namely, in *SZ* and surrounding works, as well as in his post-*SZ* work (henceforth, *early* and *later* Heidegger, respectively) – Heidegger criticizes SCS and advances ACS. The early Heidegger generally focuses his criticism on the philosophical tradition for advancing SCS, while increasingly in his later years, he comes to worry that SCS has come to guide scientific practice. Conversely, Heidegger defends ACS more explicitly in his early work but remains implicitly committed to it even in his later discussions.

Furthermore, I argue that these commitments about science inform Heidegger's views on the history of Western metaphysics and on the possibilities for human flourishing that modernity, and modern science specifically, affords.

1.1 Scope

More than fifty years have passed since the influential scholar William J. Richardson remarked, "On the longest day he ever lived, Heidegger could never be called a philosopher of science" (1968, p. 511). This remark speaks to how many used to view the notion of "Heidegger's philosophy of science" with suspicion. Perhaps Heidegger offers some insights about science, the thinking went, but his scattered remarks show him to be only vaguely interested, and at any rate, well out of date on the subject.[2]

Commentators like Joseph Kockelmans, Joseph Rouse, Trish Glazebrook, Adam Beck, and Jeff Kochan have shifted this picture substantially. It's no longer controversial to claim that Heidegger's philosophy of science is crucial to his overall project or that he offers the philosopher of science a worthy perspective. My work owes a debt to each of them.

Nevertheless, it's worth pausing to note another sense in which Richardson's remark is defensible after all: Heidegger doesn't approach science (or indeed, any other topic) in the manner characteristic of most contemporary academic philosophers.[3] Even in his most direct, sustained commentaries on science, a reader will find that Heidegger's chief concerns are not the specialized problems that dominate recent academic literature in philosophy of science (e.g., scientific realism or the logical structure of scientific explanations, let alone more granular issues, such as time measurement in climate science).

---

[2] See, e.g., Heelan (1995).   [3] Thanks to an anonymous reviewer for posing this challenge.

Heidegger occasionally argues for or suggests a position on these kinds of problems; nevertheless, he generally discusses science with his central, abiding concerns in mind: the question of being (i.e., of what being "is" as opposed to what beings are), the history of metaphysics, and the difficult position of a modern intellectual age that sits at the apex of a tradition characterized by what he calls *Seinsvergessenheit* ("forgetfulness of being" – i.e., a tendency to avoid the question of being in favor of inquiry into beings). Science, for Heidegger, is the institution that embodies modernity's answers to the questions of what knowledge is and of what is true. Investigating science thus promises to reveal how we conceive of being or knowledge, and how those conceptions sit within our broader intellectual history.

This peculiar feature of Heidegger's discussions of science poses at least two challenges with regard to the scope of the present essay. First, my discussion must consider not only Heidegger's specific claims about science, but also the connections between those claims and his broader concerns. Second, in the short space of this essay, I cannot offer a comprehensive account of Heidegger's philosophy of science. Instead, I will limit my focus to a core set of issues surrounding Heidegger's *concept* of science – i.e., his view of what science as such and in general is, as well as how that view relates to his accounts of human existence, modernity, and the history of metaphysics.

To treat those issues, I must devote significant space to Heidegger's discussions of physics, because *physicalism* (which I define in a somewhat unusually broad sense – roughly, as the privileging of physics' concepts, methods, and results in science and metaphysics[4]) figures prominently in his critiques of SCS and the history of Western metaphysics. Heidegger thinks physicalism has prevented us from understanding not only the source of science's epistemic virtue but also science's promise for human flourishing, which his preferred ACS foregrounds. But Heidegger's critique of physicalism, I argue, plays a central role within his early critique of the history of Western metaphysics, a role which most scholars have overlooked. Moreover, I argue that the later Heidegger comes to believe that the emergence of quantum physics reflects a profound shift in the aims of science that only leaves SCS more entrenched and poses serious challenges for human flourishing. Indeed, Heidegger believes that the classical-quantum shift in physics depends on, and is symptomatic of, the emergence of the set of commitments in late modernity that characterize what he calls the "age of technology."

---

[4] See Section 3.1.

Nevertheless, many key aspects of Heidegger's views on science and physics unfortunately fall outside the scope of the present essay. A (by no means exhaustive) list of such topics includes:

- Heidegger's specific views on biology, cognitive science, academic history, and so on[5]
- Heidegger's views on science in his very early (1912–1923) writings
- How Heidegger's views fit within many recent debates in philosophy of science – e.g., the role of theories vs. models in science, scientific realism, or the autonomy of science (though Sections 5–6 touch on the two latter topics)
- How Heidegger's philosophy of science relates to critical approaches like feminism or post-colonialism or to the views of his post-Kantian predecessors or later Continental thinkers – e.g., I don't treat how Heidegger intervenes in post-Kantian debates about the distinction between the *Naturwissenschaften* and *Geisteswissenschaften* (though see note 16)
- Why the early Heidegger conceives of ontology as an independent science, and why he comes to change his mind
- Heidegger's discussions of the concept of *phusis*

One final clarification is in order. Heidegger often uses "science" as a shorthand to refer to what he calls *positive science* (e.g., *SZ* 10) – i.e., the kind of domain-specific inquiry that presupposes foundational ontological assumptions that inform various specialized issues (e.g., the "three-body problem" only arises on the basis of Newtonian gravity and mechanics) – which he distinguishes from *philosophy*, or reflection on foundational ontological assumptions themselves. The implication is that Heidegger often classifies those generally referred to as groundbreaking "scientists" (e.g., Galileo, Newton, Einstein, Bohr, Heisenberg) as "philosophers."[6] Critics like Crease (2012) claim that Heidegger thus effect-ively denigrates science as (to adopt a Kuhnian idiom) "mop-up work." And this criticism is seemingly invited by remarks such as his infamous slogan "science does not think" (*WCT* 8). But as Thomson (2005, pp. 104–14) demonstrates, this slogan is just a provocative formulation of the very distinction at issue here, which Heidegger always maintains, between positive research *informed by* ontological assumptions and ontological reflection itself.[7] Crucially, however,

---

[5] On Heidegger's philosophy of biology, see Kessel (2011). Note also that, in clear homage to Dreyfus and Heidegger, Clark (1999), an important work on cognitive science, is titled *Being There*, which is the common translation for Heidegger's *Dasein*; see Clark (1999, pp. xvii, 148, 170–73).

[6] For Heidegger's appraisals of Einstein, Bohr, and Heisenberg, see *BH* 198, *CT* 67–68, *HCT* 3–4, *SZ* 9–10, *QT* 45; see also Beck (2005 pp. 168–72) on Heidegger, Einstein, and relativity. Thomson (2005, pp. 106–14) provides an excellent treatment of this distinction and its significance in Heidegger's thought.

[7] However, see Wendland (2019) for an alternative reading.

Heidegger also thinks that positive science and philosophy are structurally related – e.g., he writes that "[i]n crisis, scientific research assumes a philosophical cast" (*HCT* 3), and suggests that ontological disclosure is science's "essential task" (*P* 95). Heidegger thinks positive science is premised on a unique kind of "forgetting of being" (it makes its characteristic progress *when* and *insofar as* it is informed by a suite of ontological commitments). But it is also premised on – and, at least until late modernity, structurally occasions – a "recollection" of being (i.e., renewed ontological reflection). He thus immediately follows his remark that "science does not think" with "science always and in its own fashion has to do with thinking" (*WCT* 8).

The upshot for this essay is as follows. I will use "science" (and "scientist") in a sense broader than that of Heidegger's "positive science," because Heidegger himself believes that what he calls "philosophy" is in fact a crucial, structural aspect of mature scientific research. Thus, a consideration of Heidegger's concept of science cannot afford to exclude this aspect from the analysis. Nevertheless, I will aim to clarify the substantive point Heidegger means this distinction to track, especially when discussing Heidegger on science's biphasic (crisis/revolution—consolidation) cycle in Section 4.

1.2 Heidegger and Twentieth-Century Philosophy of Science

Heidegger bears an ambiguous relationship to contemporary philosophers of science. He criticizes the *methodological* approach to science that was popular for much of the early twentieth century. Methodological philosophers of science like Karl Popper or Imre Lakatos ask about the method that science ideally follows; this method is supposed to explain what differentiates (and perhaps elevates) science from other kinds of inquiry. But Heidegger thinks there is no common scientific method. Nevertheless, there are some interesting parallels. Heidegger thinks science is distinguished by a characteristic *ethic*, which both guides scientific practice and undergirds its epistemic virtue: science is a project dedicated to opening up access to reality, and to doing so in a unique way. And like Popper and Lakatos, Heidegger thinks science's epistemic virtue lies in its dynamism rather than its (dubiously alleged) progressive convergence on a final, true theory.

Meanwhile, commentators often note parallels between Heidegger's approach and two significant developments in twentieth-century philosophy of science: the turns toward history (see, e.g., Thomas Kuhn and Paul Feyerabend) and practice (see, e.g., Helen Longino and Bruno Latour).[8] On the former, science is

---

[8] See Kuhn (2012), Feyerabend (1993), Longino (1990), and Latour and Woolgar (1979). On the connection with Heidegger, see Glazebrook (2000, Chapters 2 and 5), Kisiel (1977), Kochan (2017), Rouse (1987, pp. 26–40), and Thomson (2005, pp. 104–15).

understood as a set of dynamic historical institutions. And a thorough historical analysis of science (including our currently cherished theories) casts doubt on triumphalist fantasies of continuous progress toward a conclusively true set of theories. Meanwhile, practice-centered thinkers tend to believe that analyzing actual scientific practices in detail, which also involves considering the institutions within which scientists work, promises to be more informative than the rational reconstruction of scientific theories or abstract consideration of scientific method that dominates much of twentieth-century philosophy of science.

In several striking respects, Heidegger anticipates these two developments. He conceives of science as a dynamic project punctuated by cyclical crises and revolutions. He thus foregrounds science's historical development, which largely occurs, he thinks, via ruptures and re-consolidations in its conceptual foundations. And his "existential" approach to science – i.e., his concept of science as a pursuit rather than as a set of theoretical results – shifts and broadens his account of what renders it epistemically salient. Moreover, his approach issues in social and (eventually) institutional analyses of scientific research.

Partially as a result of both "turns," contemporary philosophy of science is much more empirical, granular, and reticent to expound on science as such than it used to be. No doubt, much of this specialization is simply the result of academic incentives. But it also reflects the view that science isn't (and ought not be) so unified as many once thought it was (or hoped it would become). Here, too, Heidegger proves prescient: he advocates for the different fields of science to be more or less autonomous and argues against the imperialism of assumptions from physics. His arguments thus occasionally anticipate those of John Dupré, perhaps the foremost champion of the disunity-of-science thesis.[9]

But these similarities belie profound differences. Heidegger sees and extols a robust unity among the sciences. Their object domains and methods differ radically, but they all embrace, he thinks, the characteristic "ethic" to which I referred earlier. Heidegger is thus squarely interested in science as such. Although he occasionally offers an excursus on scientific history, practice, or institutions, he remains comfortable in the philosopher's armchair.[10] He spends much of his time reflecting on science's relationship to the history of philosophy and, as I'll discuss in a moment, the possibilities it offers, or fails to offer, for human flourishing.

---

[9] See Dupré (1983, 1988).
[10] For similar points, see Crease (2012), Kisiel (1977, p. 165), and Seigfried (1978, pp. 318–19).

Heidegger's idiosyncratic approach to science comes into focus when we recognize that it is consciously heir to Aristotle's analysis of the life of contemplation (the *bios theoretikos*) in *Nicomachean Ethics*.[11] For Aristotle, theoretical activity is assessed as a unique human pursuit with a special relationship to human flourishing (*eudaimonia*). He thus approaches the *bios theoretikos* on the basis of his systematic account of human existence. The *bios theoretikos* is supremely fulfilling because it exercises our lofty discursive (rational) nature, it is chosen for its own sake (unlike politics or war), and it approximates the sustained, leisurely activity that characterizes divine life.[12] Heidegger's "existential" approach to science thus is in fact *ethical* in the Aristotelian sense: it is informed by a detailed ontological analysis of human existence that uncovers the possibility for a certain kind of flourishing (what Heidegger calls "authenticity" (*Eigentlichkeit*) in *SZ*), which we attain in moments of disclosedness.[13] But Heidegger departs from Aristotle's concept of the theoretical life as static. When properly pursued, science, for Heidegger, is dynamic, and it cyclically achieves authenticity-engendering ontological disclosures. But just as surely, the clarity and fulfillment conferred by such disclosures fade. Hence, disclosures must be repeated again and again. And Heidegger eventually worries that modern science seeks to evade such disclosures altogether.

To get a better grip on Heidegger's approach, let's briefly turn to Max Weber's address "Science as a Vocation," which profoundly influenced the young Heidegger.[14] Weber observes that academic research has become, rather than a spiritual calling, an occupation much like any other – characterized by rank careerism, littered with arbitrary advantages, and so on. And it poses serious challenges to the individual hoping to gain fulfillment by it. Science is constantly in motion, developing without the prospect of concluding. Thus, any "knowledge" gained is provisional, doomed to become obsolete within a matter of years (at most). Furthermore, research becomes increasingly specialized and recondite, such that we have simultaneously sapped the world of its mystery, rendered it alien to our daily experience, and given up hope of achieving a unified, comprehensive understanding of it (hence, we have "disenchanted" it). Finally, we have lost faith that modern science (as opposed to its ancient, medieval, or early modern counterparts) will offer ethical, political, or spiritual truth.[15] So what is the researcher to do? Weber exhorts us to reconcile ourselves

---

[11] The relationship to Aristotle comes out especially in GA27 §§22–24; see also *BCAP* 5, 12, 31–32, 73, 146, 161, 185–86, 196–97; PS 114–23; *SZ* 10, 138, 172; *HCCR* 30–33.

[12] *Nicomachean Ethics* 10.7, 1177a12-1178a8.

[13] On the issue of authenticity's ethical resonance (or lack thereof), as well as its connection to *eudaimonia*, see the discussion in Section 2.3.

[14] See the excellent treatments by Crowell (1997) and Thomson (2005, pp. 94–104).

[15] Weber (2004, pp. 11–17).

to what science has become, in all its grim, mundane aspects, and to embrace the sobriety it both affords and demands.

For Heidegger, Weber foregrounds the right phenomena (the transformation of science from a rich ethical life to a mundane occupation) and asks the right question (what is this pursuit's ethical or "spiritual" significance?). But Heidegger's response sharply diverges. A proper account of human existence, he thinks, will allow us to recover a sense of science's unique ethical potential.

> *Science* is not an occupation, not a business, not a diversion, but is rather the *possibility of the existence of human beings*, and not something into which one happens by chance. (BCAP 5)

1.3 Translations, Science, and *Wissenschaft*

In general, I quote from extant translations and follow conventions for Anglophone Heidegger scholarship, but I take the liberty of revising translations on occasion. When I do so, I generally place the corresponding word or phrase in German in square brackets, especially on occasions when the departure has important implications or might arouse controversy.

One issue bears further comment. "Science" conjures images of microscopes and lab coats; and though we dub economics, sociology, anthropology (and so on) "social sciences," the term is most at home with the natural sciences. Rarely would we call history or mathematics "sciences," and fields like philosophy and literature are classed as "humanities" rather than sciences. But each of these counts as a *Wissenschaft*. So in what sense does Heidegger's analysis of *Wissenschaft* count as a philosophy of *science*?

Heidegger observes that Newtonian physics was generally recognized as a (perhaps even *the*) paradigmatic case of *Wissenschaft* in post-Kantian German philosophy – so paradigmatic that the *Geisteswissenschaften* (the humanities) look deficient by comparison.[16] Although it has a wider extension and a broader sense, Heidegger's "Wissenschaft," like our "science," refers to epistemically privileged, institutionalized research, for which physics is often seen as the exemplary case. Hence, I generally translate "Wissenschaft" as

---

[16] Heidegger's thinking makes an interesting intervention in debates among his recent predecessors over the distinction between the *Naturwissenschaften* (natural sciences) and the *Geisteswissenschaften* (the "human sciences," roughly corresponding to the "humanities" in English). It is beyond the scope of this essay to explore this connection in detail; but see Dilthey (1977) as well as the relevant selections from Windelband and Rickert in Luft (2015) for brief introductions to this topic; for relevant remarks from Heidegger, see *TDP* 25–26, 45, 64–69, 154–55; *BPWS* 40–41, 72–75, 113, 118, 155, 160, 163, 175; *PIE* 9, 118–19; *OHF* 43–45, 53–57, as well as *SZ* 152–53.

"science," and I think Heidegger's philosophy of *Wissenschaft* is indeed a philosophy of *science*.

1.4 Breakdown of Main Sections

Section 2 discusses some key concepts that inform the early Heidegger's concept of science, on which subsequent sections will draw: time and Dasein, truth, and authenticity. I also briefly outline several problems with a dominant reading of the early Heidegger's philosophy of science centered on the concept of presence-at-hand.

Section 3 examines Heidegger's critique of physicalism. I detail Heidegger's basic objections: physicalism collapses ontological distinctions, threatens the autonomy of other fields, and distorts our understanding of science by promoting SCS. I then consider his genealogical analysis of physicalism: it depends, Heidegger argues, on a dogmatic commitment to ancient Greek metaphysics, which privileges entities characterized by complete, constant presence.

Section 4 unpacks how Heidegger promotes ACS via his "existential" approach that relates science to his concepts of truth and authenticity. Science, for Heidegger, is the pursuit of truth, but in a unique sense: it is the commitment to opening up access to reality *projectively*, *thematically*, and *objectively*, and to renewing that access cyclically when crises emerge. I discuss why Heidegger thinks scientific crises demand fresh ontological disclosures that, in turn, demand researchers who achieve authenticity.

Section 5 takes up Heidegger's later discussions of science, which, despite their growing pessimism, are premised on the same core commitments as his earlier discussions. Heidegger worries that SCS is gaining currency over ACS not only in the philosophy of science, but in scientific practice as well. After briefly analyzing Heidegger's slogan "science is the theory of the actual," I spend the rest of the section discussing Heidegger's critique of how the "industry" (*Betrieb*) of science incentivizes scientists to avoid ontological inquiry. The result, Heidegger fears, is that science proper will dissolve and become, de facto, a species of engineering.

Section 6 unpacks Heidegger's dialogue with Werner Heisenberg on the significance of quantum physics for science, metaphysics, and intellectual history more broadly. Heisenberg thinks quantum physics undermines the objective study of nature that motivated classical physics, and that in doing so, it betokens a new, anxiety-inducing historical epoch. I argue that Heidegger positively appropriates Heisenberg's claims: the classical-quantum shift betokens a shift in the "history of being" from the early modern age to the age of technology. But these joint revolutionary developments, he believes, further entrench SCS over ACS. I close by considering Heidegger's concerns about the ethical implications of quantum physics and the age of technology.

2 Key Concepts for the Early Heidegger's Approach to Science

Below, I discuss several important concepts that figure in Heidegger's philosophy of science in *SZ*: time and Dasein, truth, and authenticity. I close by briefly identifying several problems with a dominant reading of Heidegger's philosophy of science centered on the concept of presence-at-hand (*Vorhandenheit*).

2.1 Time and Dasein

Heidegger presents a notoriously forbidding analysis of temporality in *SZ* §§61–83. My discussion here sidesteps this important but thorny analysis.[17] Instead, key for me is Heidegger's (comparatively straightforward) guiding insight about the relationship between ontological and temporal concepts. Even this simple insight is crucial for understanding what Heidegger thinks is distinctive about human existence and the lacunae in the Western philosophical tradition.

Different kinds of things bear different relationships to time, and these temporal distinctions have taken on ontological significance in the philosophical tradition. For instance, Plato, Aristotle, and countless theologians think ontologically superior things (forms, the heavenly bodies, God) are distinguished by their eternal stability, as opposed to inferior things, which are subject to change and time's passage.[18] Similarly, mathematical things (numbers, theorems, and so on) are thought to be, as Heidegger puts it, distinctively "extratemporal" (*HCT* 5).[19]

Heidegger enters into a critical dialogue with the tradition: he too articulates ontological distinctions with the help of temporal concepts, but he also means to question how the tradition has privileged certain temporal concepts – and with them, certain kinds of things – over others. (Section 3 examines this claim at length.)

At this point, we must discuss Heidegger's concept of *Dasein* (literally, "being-there," or, as Dahlstrom argues, "being-here"[20]), which refers to the class of entities traditionally conceived as "rational" or "minded," of which

---

[17] But see Dahlstrom (1995) and Blattner (1999) for key treatments of these issues.

[18] See Plato, *Phaedo* 74aff.; Aristotle, *Nicomachean Ethics* 10.7–10.9, 1177a11–1179a34 and *Metaphysics* 12.6–12.7, 1071b3–1073a13; Augustine, *Confessions* 11.13.15–11.13.16; Maimonides, *Guide for the Perplexed*, Part I, Chapter LV; and Aquinas, *Summa Contra Gentiles*, Book 1, Chapters 13 and 15.

[19] See also *SZ* 18.

[20] Dahlstrom (2001, pp. xxiii–xxvi); see, however, the objections by Sheehan (unpublished manuscript) and Hemming (2013, pp. 10, 29–31, 170–72).

humans are the paradigmatic and perhaps indeed the only members. Note that humanity and Dasein are not co-extensive (e.g., humans in vegetative states are not instances of Dasein; human physiological events *per se* aren't events of Dasein). I sometimes use "humanity," "human existence," (etc.) interchangeably with "Dasein," but readers should bear in mind this caveat.

Heidegger offers his own definition of this class. "*Understanding of being is itself a definite characteristic of Dasein's being.* Dasein is ontically distinctive in that it *is* ontological" (*SZ* 12). In other words, *Dasein* refers to beings who are capable of ontology. Let me elaborate. The spatial resonance of *da* (here, there) indicates that for us – unlike for nonhuman animals, minerals, and vegetables – other things' existence (as well as our own) is a phenomenon. We perceive things in the world and, just as importantly, we can perceive *that* they exist and *how* they exist. We make ontological distinctions simply by dint of navigating everyday life (e.g., we distinguish wildlife from pets, my stuff from your stuff, the living from the dead). And when prompted, we can articulate those distinctions more or less cogently.

Heidegger thinks Dasein has a peculiar relationship to time. In traditional Christian theology, God is, to borrow a grammatical term, *perfective* (fully present at every moment, lacking in nothing). Dasein, by contrast, is *imperfective* – processual, or structurally incomplete; it "*is* ... that which ... it is *not yet*" (*SZ* 145). That is to say, a thorough account of us must refer to things that we lack at any given present moment. For instance, my dog Luna is an important part of my life. But having a dog means assuming a suite of standing obligations that I cannot completely discharge at any given moment. Having Luna structures my activities and emotions across an undefined stretch of my future, and it involves me in various relationships (e.g., with my spouse, Luna's veterinarian, her kibble manufacturer, etc.). This imperfective relationship toward the future is an example of what Heidegger calls *projection* (*Entwurf*).[21] When we project, our experiences are pre-structured in accordance with some *existential possibility* – i.e., a possible way of existing – of higher or lower order (having a dog versus walking the dog; being the primary household cook versus cooking tonight's dinner). For instance, when I project upon the possibility of making a fresh pasta dinner, certain objects, places, activities, and relationships become salient: a cookbook, pot, and pasta roller; my kitchen and a well-stocked pantry; hours of prior practice; those who taught me various techniques and my spouse who feeds the pasta into the roller while I pull and lay it out.

Note that while individual projections may end, projection itself is never complete; finishing the meal means that a new project begins (eating, cleaning up, re-stocking, etc.). Death alone puts an end to projecting, but it also puts an end

---

[21] *SZ* 145.

to *me*. We, for Heidegger, have this peculiar relationship to time: we ceaselessly project into the future; we are intrinsically dynamic and imperfective.

2.2 Truth

Anglophone academic philosophy has generally analyzed truth via the truth predicate.[22] In this tradition, the central question is what it means for a proposition (or a belief, sentence, etc.) to be true or false.[23] But as Wrathall (2011, pp. 43–44) points out, this question isn't of primary concern to Heidegger. When it comes up, he accepts some version of the correspondence theory without much ado.[24]

Heidegger's concept of truth is instead premised on other uses of "true" and "truth," especially cases where we attribute truth to entities ("a true friend") or when "truth" takes on an ethical resonance ("speak truth to power"). Thus, Heidegger supplements but doesn't supplant the familiar truth-predicate discourse.[25] Nevertheless, as we will see presently, Heidegger thinks these other senses of truth are structurally related to the truth predicate, and he worries that the dominance of truth-predicate analysis pushes these other – and, as he sees it, more fundamental – aspects of truth to the margins.

Heidegger claims that, at least since the nineteenth century, German philosophy has conceived of truth within the narrow limits of the truth predicate.[26] I henceforth refer to this aspect of truth as *propositional truth*. The target of Heidegger's critique is what Dahlstrom calls *the logical prejudice*: "the notion that propositional truth is the most elementary sort of truth" (2001, p. 385). In other words, the logical prejudice claims that an account of propositional truth more or less exhausts a philosophical account of truth.[27]

Heidegger disagrees. Take, for instance, the proposition *Paul's laptop is silver*. This proposition has a truth value; but to understand or evaluate it, we must first be acquainted with the entities it references (my laptop, the color silver). Heidegger's term for this *ontic* acquaintance is *uncovering*

---

[22] This section bears a significant debt to Dahlstrom (2001) and Wrathall (2011).

[23] Consider that as of this writing, the *Stanford Encyclopedia of Philosophy*'s entry on "Truth" (Glanzberg 2021) is solely devoted to truth-predicate analysis; and the typical menu of "theories of truth" – correspondence, coherence, pragmatist, and disquotationalist – all concern the truth predicate. See also Dahlstrom (2001, pp. 24–28).

[24] See Wrathall (1999) and Wrathall (2011, pp. 18–19, 43). Carman (2007) discusses an interesting wrinkle in Heidegger's relationship with the correspondence theory.

[25] Tugendhat (1994) famously claims that Heidegger undermines a traditional understanding of the truth predicate (see also the positive re-appraisals of Tugendhat's critique offered by Lafont (2000, pp. 115–24, 146–49) and Smith (2007)). But see the effective replies by Dahlstrom (2001, pp. 397–407) and Wrathall (2011, pp. 34–39).

[26] As Dahlstrom argues (2001, pp. 1–47; see esp. pp. 35–36), Heidegger traces the roots of this tendency to the influential nineteenth-century Platonist philosopher Rudolph Hermann Lotze. See *LQT* 22–23, 52ff.; see also Lotze (2015) for a brief but relevant selection.

[27] See Dahlstrom (2001, p. 19).

(*Entdeckung*). Note also that a particular object cannot be uncovered for me unless I have some acquaintance with what it means to be an object of that kind (what a laptop or color is). Heidegger's term for this *ontological* acquaintance is *disclosedness* (*Erschlossenheit*). Disclosedness and uncovering are, therefore, necessary conditions of our ability to understand and evaluate propositional truth. Heidegger's concept of truth hinges on these phenomena of uncovering and, more fundamentally, disclosedness. Henceforth, I refer to this aspect of truth as *disclosed truth*. Disclosed truth is supposed to ground rather than negate propositional truth. "Assertion," he writes, "is not the primary 'locus' of truth. *On the contrary* . . . assertion is grounded in Dasein's uncovering or rather in its *disclosedness*" (*SZ* 226).

Let me close by noting two crucial differences between propositional truth and disclosed truth. First, they have different temporal orientations. A proposition's truth value is eternal. *Two plus two equals four* is true now and forever. But being's disclosedness is ephemeral and historical: people were not acquainted with laptops until the late twentieth century; electrons went unnoticed until the late nineteenth century. Heidegger is intensely interested in the historicity of disclosures, i.e., in understanding how whole realms of things enter or exit our perceptual orbit.

Second, and structurally related to the first, is something Wrathall (2011, pp. 1–2, 17–18) highlights: Heidegger generally uses privative words (*un*cover-ing, *un*concealment, *a*letheia) to characterize disclosed truth. Each bespeaks a more basic concealment. This implication isn't supposed to be an artifact of language: Heidegger thinks that disclosed truth is a privative phenomenon. As he writes,

> only in so far as Dasein has been disclosed has it also been closed off; and only in so far as entities within the world have been uncovered along with Dasein, have such entities, as possibly encounterable within-the-world, been covered up (hidden) or disguised. (*SZ* 222[28])

Heidegger means at least two things here. First, the disclosure or uncovering of any given phenomenon is structurally dependent on the concealing of other phenomena. For instance, insofar as we focus on the two-dimensional area of a strip of land, we allow its other features (e.g., its beauty, arability, or history) to recede into the background; in a similar vein, Nietzsche contends that egalitar-ian assumptions lead us to ignore (or downplay) the various inequalities among humans that were of paramount significance for the ancient Greeks.[29]

---

[28] See also *OBT* 23, 29–31.   [29] Nietzsche (1974, p. 91).

Heidegger's frequently invoked metaphor of the "clearing" (*Lichtung*) highlights this structural dependence of disclosure on concealment.[30]

Second, Heidegger notes a tendency for disclosures to lapse over time, either because they have been forgotten or replaced or, more insidiously, because they have become so taken for granted that we have lost their original sense.[31] For instance, MacIntyre (2007) famously worries that various assumptions, over time, have led to modern Western philosophers losing the ability to have successful ethical discourse; as we will discuss in Section 3.3, Heidegger thinks that the equation of being with constant presence has become so taken for granted in the West that we have lost a sense of its original motivation. Note, then, that any given instance of disclosure or uncovering is not eternally secure but, rather, must be repeated time and again. "It is therefore essential," he writes, "that Dasein should explicitly appropriate what has already been uncovered, defend it *against* semblance and disguise, and assure itself of its uncoveredness again and again" (*SZ* 222).

Disclosed truth's privative nature highlights the ethical salience of Heidegger's concept of truth: we must constantly work to achieve and maintain our acquaintance with things. All of us, most of the time, remain within the narrow limits of intelligibility furnished by society. Disclosures require painstaking effort, and are never final: most truths are undiscovered, and those that have been discovered inevitably fade into insignificance or obscurity.[32] But Heidegger worries that the logical prejudice, by foregrounding propositional truth and ignoring disclosed truth, offers the comforting delusion that truth, once discovered, is secure.

2.3 Authenticity

Heidegger's notion of authenticity poses significant interpretive challenges. But its first appearance in *SZ* furnishes perhaps Heidegger's most straightforward remarks: Dasein "*can*, in its very being, 'choose' itself and win itself"; in so doing, Dasein achieves *authenticity* (*Eigentlichkeit*). Conversely, Dasein can also be *inauthentic*, or "lose itself and never win itself; or only 'seem' to do so" (*SZ* 42).[33]

---

[30] See, e.g., *SZ* 130, *OBT* 29–31; see also Wrathall's helpful discussion (2011, pp. 32–34).

[31] The discussion of "historical falling" in Section 3 elaborates on this tendency.

[32] Heidegger's extended analysis of Plato's allegory of the cave (*ET* 17–68) underscores these points.

[33] My account of authenticity bears a significant debt to Carman's (2005) remarkably cogent and concise analysis of authenticity. Unlike Carman, however, I think the distinction between second- and third-person stances toward oneself is relevant to Heidegger's concept. A robust development of my account might also consider Martin Buber's distinction between the self-concepts contained in I-You and I-It stances (see, e.g., 1996, pp. 80–82, 111–15). Note also that

Note thus that "authenticity" names a specific good that Dasein can achieve – and this is so notwithstanding Heidegger's occasional protests that his analysis of authenticity serves primarily to round out his descriptive account of the existential analytic of Dasein, and that neither it nor any other concept is offered primarily in service to an ethics. But an ambiguity lurks in these protests. Contrast (1) "ethics" qua a descriptive account of the human good premised on a detailed analysis of human existence (*à la* Aristotle) with (2) "ethics" qua an analysis of moral prescriptions (*à la* Bentham or Kant). I contend that Heidegger's protests primarily concern (2); indeed, he sometimes suggests that Aristotle's ethics in fact constitutes an existential analytic of Dasein – i.e., the same kind of project he pursues in *SZ*. "One cannot force Greek ethics," he writes, "into the mode of questioning of modern ethics . . . Dasein was simply seen there with regard to its possibility of being as such" (*PS* 122).[34] Heidegger's notion of authenticity thus indeed has ethical significance in this broader, Aristotelian sense. Moreover, I argue that authenticity, for Heidegger, functions in a role that partially parallels Aristotle's *eudaimonia* – indeed, Heidegger even writes in *PS* that *eudaimonia*, for Aristotle, "constitutes the authenticity of the being [*Eigentlichkeit des Seins*] of human Dasein" (118). The parallel shouldn't be overstated; we will see that Heideggerian authenticity is both more specific and more fragile than Aristotelian *eudaimonia*, which denotes an overall and robust state of well-being, encompassing virtuous action *and* good fortune.[35] Nevertheless, like *eudaimonia*, Heideggerian authenticity constitutes a specific kind of flourishing – or, as Taylor Carman writes, (though without reference to *eudaimonia*) "a desirable or choice-worthy mode of existence" (2005, p. 286).

The specific good that "authenticity" names concerns *self-ownership*, as indeed the German word *Eigentlichkeit*, with its root *eigen* (own), suggests. On my reading, we achieve authenticity when we take ownership of ourselves amid the social norms that structure our lives by adopting a thoroughly first-person stance toward ourselves. When inauthentic, by contrast, we evade self-ownership by adopting a third-person stance toward ourselves. Such a stance, importantly, does *not* primarily involve considering the perspective of someone whom we specifically care about and find ourselves in relationship with – we might call that a *second-person* stance toward ourselves. Rather, it means

---

there are significant interpretive and philosophical controversies about this notion that it is beyond the bounds of this essay to explore. The interested reader might consult Guignon (1993) for an account of authenticity related to the notion of "narrative continuity" (230); McManus (2019) for a reading based on the notion of an "all-things-considered judgment"; and Käufer's (2021) helpful overview of the concept, which also begins by citing these same remarks from *SZ* 42.

[34] See also *PS* 90, 123; *P* 268–71.   [35] *Nicomachean Ethics* 1097a15-21, 1099b9-1101b9.

considering how we measure up to a more or less abstract sense of how *one* should act, which means with how we measure up to prevailing social norms.

Heidegger thinks that we are generally inauthentic. Largely, we take care to do what *one* does with more or less turbulence (e.g., one brushes one's teeth twice a day). And simply to rebel against the norm is only to underscore its current authority. In either case, we relate to ourselves third-personally, as someone whose life is measured against social norms, and so we pass off responsibility for our actions (and feelings, impulses, and so on) to the social norms from which we regard ourselves. Heidegger thus calls my everyday self a "one"-self rather than my *own* self. Meanwhile, he calls our tendency toward inauthenticity *falling* (*Verfallen*), i.e., the tendency passively to accept the authority of prevailing social norms.[36] But how do we achieve authenticity? And why do we fall into inauthenticity?

Social norms are contingent but ineluctable: for instance, contemporary American norms are different from those in medieval Japan, and it is pure chance that I happen to live in twenty-first-century America rather than medieval Japan. Yet I can no more become a samurai than I can sprout wings and fly. It's a contingent fact that a community happens to abide by these norms rather any of the other infinite possibilities. Nevertheless, none of us has the power to ignore our social norms. We are socialized into them before we can articulate any objections and, once we can, it's too late – our discourse, habits, social relationships, and pursuits have been irrevocably shaped. Nevertheless, social norms are generic, and hence, necessarily underdetermine specific actions – the "one," writes Heidegger, "has always stolen away whenever Dasein presses for a decision" (*SZ* 127). Social norms inexorably structure our deliberations but can't settle them. And they are also dynamic: although we can't arbitrarily slough off their influence, we can nevertheless creatively "reply" (*erwidert*) to them, and hence, contribute to the emergence of new possibilities (*SZ* 383–86). We thus are "forced to be free": each of us bears an inalienable responsibility for our actions (a phenomenon that Heidegger refers to as our existential *guilt* or *responsibility* (*Schuld*)[37]).

For instance, in modern America, we learn the norm *prioritize work*. So what should you do when in the middle of a shift you hear that your child is sick and needs to be picked up from school? To leave might jeopardize your job. Then again, another norm we learn is *prioritize family*. Someone needs to pick up your child, and who better than *you*, their parent? So which norm takes priority? Deciding in this manner is palpably alienating; we feel that whatever action we take is dictated to us by these underdetermined social norms.[38]

---

[36] See esp. *SZ* §§35–38.   [37] See *SZ* §58.

When we evade responsibility, we are inauthentic. And inauthenticity is suboptimal: it leaves us deceived (we falsely believe that prevailing norms are responsible for our actions) and powerless (by passively acquiescing to extant social norms, our possible actions are especially constrained by them).

Authenticity, by contrast, liberates us. We achieve authenticity when we embrace our existential responsibility, a phenomenon which Heidegger calls *resoluteness* (*Entschlossenheit*).[39] And we embrace our responsibility when we *anticipate* our "death" in Heidegger's peculiar existential sense.[40] Crucially, to anticipate death does not mean to recognize the fact that, like everyone else, we too will die someday (and be buried, mourned, forgotten, etc.), or even to dwell on the fact that my death in the ordinary sense (which Heidegger calls "demise") appears empirically certain (*SZ* 257–58). Rather, anticipating death means recognizing that all my pursuits face the latent threat of dissolution (whether because they encounter an obstacle, prove impracticable, or lose their grip on me). I recognize that my activities, habits, feelings, relationships, and so on – in short, all aspects of my identity – are subject to contingency, change, and destruction. Heidegger thus writes that death "*is possible at any moment*" (*SZ* 258) and stresses that "Dasein is dying as long as it exists" (*SZ* 251; see also *SZ* 254, 259).

Anticipating our death, Heidegger thinks, forces me to adopt a thoroughly first-person relationship to myself, because I recognize a threat to *my own* existence. It thus discloses my existential responsibility. Social norms cannot be pushed aside, but we can creatively respond to them rather than passively acquiescing to them: we can see that they too are contingent and fragile, we can catch sight of new possibilities, and we can decide when to defy or accept.

Given that authenticity is optimal, why does Heidegger think that it is relatively rare? At least part of the answer is that falling and inauthenticity are, as Heidegger remarks, "tempting" and "tranquilizing" (*SZ* 177), while authenticity, born of existential *anxiety* and *uncanniness*, is burdensome.

We feel anxiety when we recognize our existential responsibility. *I* am forced to act amid social norms and within a situation that is largely beyond my control. No authoritative guidance is to be found – we would be responsible even for the decision to follow any proffered guidance.[41] My decisions are consequential: being *projectival*, they will pre-structure my experiences across an indefinite stretch of time.[42] And my pursuits are all subject to an insuperable threat of dissolution.

---

[38] On alienation, see *SZ* 178.   [39] See especially *SZ* §60.

[40] See Carman (2005, pp. 290–91) for a helpful and concise account of Heidegger's concept of existential death.

[41] Sartre (2007, pp. 33–34) famously unpacks this claim.

Anxiety discloses the latent *uncanniness* or *eeriness* (*Unheimlichkeit*) of our existence.[43] Moments ago, the world appeared ordinary and obvious (before hearing about your child's illness, it was an ordinary day at work), and most people apparently find it unproblematic (your coworkers and customers are going about their business). But we now recognize it as deeply questionable. Whereas before there seemed to be an obvious course of action (handling orders, sweeping up, catching up with coworkers), we now recognize that innumerable actions are possible.[44] Anxiety thus is destabilizing; but for that reason, it shakes us out of our prior falling and allows us to achieve authenticity. It forces us to attend with fresh eyes to the particulars of our concrete situation in making our decision rather than filtering our perception and deliberation through generic, ossified norms.[45] Say you decide to stay at work and find a relative to pick up your child. You recognize that others might harshly judge your action, but you can accept this because you've taken ownership of your choice. (You recognize, perhaps, that losing your job would harm your child most of all.)

I noted earlier that Dasein, for Heidegger, is processual or structurally incomplete. We now can sharpen this point: Dasein's existence consists of a biphasic cycle, where we *fall* from authenticity into inauthenticity. We must *repeatedly retrieve* (*wiederholen*) our authentic selves; we never attain a perfect or permanent authenticity. Why do we find ourselves in this cycle? The best answer we get from Heidegger is that authenticity-engendering resolute decisions are made in the face of death – i.e., in the face of the acknowledgment that all of my pursuits will dissolve. The dissolution is total and permanent in the case of my demise; but we also experience dissolution in daily life when my pursuits fail or when I cease to identify with them. A resolute decision thus demands that "one *holds oneself free for* the possibility of *taking it back*" – and "[i]n its death," Heidegger adds, "Dasein must simply 'take back' everything" (*SZ* 308). Authenticity is thus necessarily ephemeral; it must be repeated again and again as my pursuits dissolve for one reason or another.[46] Eventually, we find ourselves "going through the motions," passively doing what "one" would do, and hence, existing in the mode of inauthenticity.

---

[42] See Section 2.1. [43] See *SZ* 188–89; see also *IPR* 220–21, 240–41.

[44] Withy (2015) helpfully unpacks the distinction between feeling and being uncanny, and, relatedly, between uncanniness as an occasional versus as a general condition.

[45] *SZ* 299–300, 307–308. Heidegger's notion of the concrete situation (*Situation*) as opposed to the generic character of social norms is informed by Aristotle's analysis of *phronesis* in *Nicomachean Ethics* 6. See *PS* 15–123 for Heidegger's lengthy analysis of *phronesis*; Dreyfus (2004) and Carman (2005, pp. 291–92) offer helpful commentary.

[46] *SZ* 308.

2.4 The Red Herring of Presence-at-Hand

Scholars have generally held that Heidegger thinks science privileges the study of entities that instantiate a mode of being he dubs *Vorhandenheit* (typically translated as "presence-at-hand").[47]

Presence-at-hand is an ontological concept that, along with its counterpart, readiness-to-hand (*Zuhandenheit*), characterizes entities that are distinct from Dasein. I'll say more about presence-at-hand in Section 3; for now, Table 1 summarizes this threefold distinction.[48]

I think the dominant interpretation of Heidegger's philosophy of science is false, and importantly so. Heidegger believes classical and modern physics (henceforth, *post-Scholastic physics*) privilege presence-at-hand, and that science only under the distorting influence and guise of *physicalism* privileges presence-at-hand. Crucially, therefore, Heidegger thinks that neither science nor natural science proper privileges presence-at-hand.

Given the standard interpretation's dominance, properly refuting it would require a sustained treatment that would take us beyond the scope of this project. But let me briefly list the main problems it confronts.

Problem 1. One of the most significant through lines of Heidegger's career is an emphasis on ontological differentiation, i.e., an insistence that reality is furnished not only with different things but radically different *kinds* of things. Indeed, we can profitably read Heidegger as a critic of the Quinean "taste for desert landscapes" (2004, p. 179). It therefore is tenuous to attribute

Table 1 Dasein, readiness-to-hand, and presence-at-hand.

	Dasein	**Readiness-to-hand**	**Presence-at-hand**
Description	being capable of doing ontology	being a tool, or a means to some end	being simply on hand, independent of Dasein
Examples	humans	hammers, cups	rocks, clouds

---

[47] See, e.g., Beck (2002, p. 107; 2005, pp. 173–74), Blattner (1995, p. 322), Brandom (1983, p. 387), Brandom (1997, p. 34), Caputo (2012, p. 268), Dreyfus (1991, pp. 79–84), Kockelmans (1985, pp. 125, 204), McNeill (1999, pp. 80–85), Rouse (1985a, p. 200), and Rouse (2005, pp. 178, 180–81). Glazebrook (2000, pp. 8–9, 17, 63, 97–98) and Kochan (2017, pp. 61–65) don't explicitly endorse this view but nevertheless strongly suggest support for it. Note that Caputo, Kockelmans, Blattner, McNeill, Brandom, and especially Beck identify shortcomings with a wide interpretation of this claim; but they ultimately endorse a narrower interpretation.

[48] Note that I intend the kind of objects referenced in Table 1 in their normal instantiations; we also can treat such objects differently from these typical ontological categories (for instance, slavery treats humans as ready-to-hand).

to him a view of science as ontologically homogeneous, especially since he views his own project (at this point in his career) as scientific.[49]

Problem 2. The two chief arguments for the dominant interpretation fail. These arguments turn, respectively, on Heidegger's analysis of equipmental breakdowns in *SZ* §16 and theoretical assertions in *SZ* §33.[50] I point out some of the chief difficulties in Goldberg (2021); my refutation of the latter argument parallels claims advanced in Golob (2013).

Problem 3. Heidegger unambiguously states that biology, economics, and history do not (or at least, ought not) privilege presence-at-hand.[51] It is therefore unclear which sciences besides physics, in his view, do in fact properly privilege presence-at-hand.

Problem 4. Most key passages cited in support of the dominant interpretation suggest a connection between science and presence-at-hand. But when read more carefully, we can see that most of Heidegger's discussions concern physics specifically rather than science as such.[52]

Problem 5. Heidegger claims that modern science and metaphysics is physicalistic, and he is a dogged critic of physicalism. These facts amplify the significance of Problems (3) and (4). In fact, Heidegger's diagnosis and critique of modernity as physicalistic, to which I now turn, is fundamental not only to his concept of science but also to his early critique of the history of Western metaphysics.

3 Heidegger's Critique of Physicalism in *Being and Time*

Below, I present Heidegger's critique of physicalism by addressing three questions: (3.1) What is physicalism? (3.2) What is wrong with physicalism? And (3.3) what is physicalism's historical origin?

---

[49] *BPP* 15–19.

[50] Proponents of the former interpretation include Blattner (1995, pp. 322–25), Dreyfus (1991, pp. 46–54, 59, 60–70, 78–87, 120–24), Guignon (1983, pp. 100–102, 150–58), Kockelmans (1985, pp. 118–25, 204–5), and Rouse (1985a, pp. 201–2). Proponents of the latter interpretation include Brandom (1983, 1997) and Rouse (2005).

[51] See, respectively, *SZ* 46, 49–50, 58, 194, 246–47; 361; and *SZ* 381–82, 388–89, 392–93, 395.

[52] The best prima facie evidence concerns Heidegger's discussion of science in *SZ* §69b; but he claims (p. 361) that his discussion concerns physics specifically rather than science as such (see also his "restriction" on p. 357).

3.1 What Is Physicalism?

Physicalism (or *Physikalismus*) is a term that Heidegger rarely uses.[53] Nevertheless, it names a principal target of his critique of modern metaphysics and philosophy of science.

In the current academic literature, "physicalism" usually refers to the position in metaphysics which holds that everything is physical. I will henceforth call this position *ontological physicalism* (OP) and reserve "physicalism" for a broader package of commitments that includes OP as well as three other claims. All four claims are suggested by the view that physics – its concepts, methods, and results – is the privileged mode of inquiry (see Table 2).

Note that "physics" here refers to both classical and modern physics. Besides his occasional qualified praise of Einstein, the early Heidegger does not comment much on the emerging modern physics.[54] At this point, he believes that his analysis, generally directed at classical physics, applies *mutatis mutandis* to modern physics.[55] Classical physics gives birth to the mathematization of nature, which modern physics, for all its innovations, carries forward.

Henceforth, "physicalism," unless otherwise specified and with few exceptions, refers to the cluster of these four claims. They are not mutually entailing,

Table 2 Four claims of physicalism.

Ontological Physicalism (OP)	All things, or at least the truly fundamental things, are physical.
Methodological Physicalism (MP)	Researchers in other fields ought to appropriate the methods and concepts of physics as much as possible. Biology, psychology, sociology, and so on ought, as much as possible, to treat their objects as instances of physical kinds and to render explanations consistent with prevailing physics.
Physics' Exemplary Status (PES)	Physics ought uniquely to serve as a model for the other sciences to emulate.
Physics' Primacy (PP)	Physics' claims have priority over those of the other sciences. If another science's postulate P conflicts with a postulate of physics P^*, we should *prima facie* be skeptical of P rather than P^*.

---

[53] But see *BCAP* 271.   [54] See note 6.

[55] As we will see (Section 6), the later Heidegger comes to doubt this view as he considers the implications of quantum theory.

but they are mutually supportive. For instance, OP is perhaps the chief motivation for the other three; meanwhile, PP provides prima facie motivation for MP, as does MP for PES. We will see that Heidegger denies all four claims.

3.2 What Is Wrong with Physicalism?

Heidegger's primary objection is to OP; he thinks it collapses genuine ontological distinctions. For instance, Heidegger frequently stresses that physicalism collapses the distinction between Dasein and physical nature. Section 3.2.1 unpacks this complaint.

Heidegger has another basic commitment about science that, when combined with his primary objection to OP, renders MP, PES, and PP implausible: each science should operate autonomously. Section 3.2.2 elaborates on these claims.

I also cover two further objections. In Section 3.2.3, I discuss Heidegger's claim that physicalism distorts our understanding of science (objection to MP, PES), and Section 3.2.4 canvasses his view that physicalism emerges as the result of an epistemically unreliable process that I call *historical falling* (objection to OP, MP, PES, PP).

3.2.1 Not Everything Is Physical

OP collapses one of the most salient ontological distinctions of all: Dasein versus physical nature.[56] Dasein, for Heidegger, is not physical – not in the sense that Dasein violates the laws of physics but, rather, in the sense that Dasein is not the sort of thing that physical concepts describe.[57] If a revolution in physics were to occur, then our understanding of matter and energy would radically shift while our understanding of Dasein would remain untouched.

For Heidegger, Dasein is unique in forming sophisticated, discursively mediated relationships with entities (ourselves, others, nature, tools, sacred texts or artifacts, and so on). But if one conceives of Dasein as, ultimately, a species of the physical, this unique feature becomes, at most, an object of genetic explanation. For instance, consider anxiety. "Anxiety," he writes,

> is often conditioned by 'physiological' factors. This fact ... is a problem ontologically, not merely with regard to its ontical causation and development. Only because Dasein is anxious in the very depths of its being, does it become possible for anxiety to be elicited physiologically. (SZ 190)

---

[56] See *SZ* 13 on Dasein's significance.
[57] Of course, the human body is the sort of thing that the concepts of physics describe; but recall that the categories of Dasein and humanity are not equivalent. (See Section 2.1.)

Heidegger here acknowledges that we can explain the physiological genesis of anxiety (say, it is occasioned by a surplus of epinephrine or a deficit of serotonin). But these genetic accounts say nothing about what anxiety is: an unsettling mood. What does anxiety disclose – what kinds of things does it put us in touch with? How do we relate to those things when anxious versus when not anxious? Genetic accounts don't address these questions; instead, they presuppose answers to them. We can look for the physiological correlates of anxiety only after we have identified what anxiety is. If OP were true, then an exhaustive description of the physical process that occasions anxiety just would be a thorough description of anxiety. But that's not the case: such an account would leave the aforementioned basic questions untouched.

Similarly, Heidegger argues that the notion of *equipmental place* is neither identical nor reducible to the concepts of space in classical and modern physics. Heidegger writes that "[e]quipment has its *place*, or else it 'lies around'; this must be distinguished in principle from just occurring at random in some spatial position" (*SZ* 102). Heidegger means to indicate here how every item of equipment *belongs* somewhere – for instance, my set of keys belongs either on the keychain hooks by my front door (when I'm at home) or in my backpack or front pocket (when I'm on the go). These places are real features of ready-to-hand equipment, but they are "not ascertained . . . by the observational measurement of space" (*SZ* 103). My keys' location makes no difference to them qua physical objects; but it makes all the difference to them qua items of equipment. When I leave them somewhere else, they are palpably *out of place*. Indeed, Heidegger writes that the "pure homogeneous space" of classical physics, wherein objects can occupy any arbitrary position within a three-dimensional totality, "shows itself only when . . . the worldly character of the ready-to-hand gets specifically *deworlded*," which results in "a context of extended things which are present-at-hand and no more" (*SZ* 112). More broadly, in *SZ* §§21–24, Heidegger argues that there is a whole package of spatial features, including but not limited to place, that is operative in our daily existence with ready-to-hand entities (which he refers to as "Dasein's spatiality"). These features are neither equivalent nor reducible to the spatial features of present-at-hand physical objects.

3.2.2 Each Science Should Operate Autonomously

Heidegger thinks each science should operate more or less autonomously. He believes that scientific research ought to be pursued solely with reference to its specific subject matter. Methods appropriate for one science will likely not be appropriate for others. "All evidence," he writes, "is . . . geared to a corresponding region of subject matter. It is absurd to want to transpose one possibility of evidence, for example, the mathematical, into other kinds of apprehension" (*HCT* 50).[58]

When combined with his view that we should not assume that any given subject matter is identical (or reducible) to some restricted domain of physics (recall Section 3.2.1), MP, PES, and PP become untenable. Scientists should not uniquely emulate physics, prioritize its claims, or adopt its methods and concepts. (Indeed, Heidegger often stresses that historians and psychologists run into trouble when they take their bearings from physics.[59]) Two cases from the history of science offer limited support for Heidegger's contention.

The first concerns evolutionary biology, which failed to get off the ground for decades after the publication of *On the Origin of Species* in part because it ran into the buzz saw of physics: later nineteenth-century models indicated that the earth was far too young to allow natural selection to yield the organismic diversity and complexity that we observe. Because of PP, Kelvin's physics stymied Darwinian biology.[60]

The second example concerns genetics.[61] Barbara McClintock discovered genetic transposition by working extensively with maize in the 1940s and presented her findings to her colleagues beginning in the 1950s. Biologists now accept that transposition is a pervasive phenomenon, and McClintock is recognized as a groundbreaking researcher.[62] But for decades, her research was dismissed. A key reason was the physicalist midcentury turn that occurred in the midst of what's often called the "molecular revolution" in biology. Under the leadership of the trained physicist Max Delbrück, geneticists sought out simplifying models and general laws, and a core assumption was the stability of the genome. Because McClintock's research undermined that assumption and postulated a dynamic organism-genome relationship, her work was generally viewed with suspicion. But McClintock's now-legendary attentiveness to her subject matter allowed her to avoid succumbing to the physicalist scruples that were then dominant, which failed to account for the gene regulation events that McClintock routinely observed. Physicalism prejudiced McClintock's colleagues against accepting her results and thus hindered an important area of biological research.

---

[58] See also *SZ* 8–10, 361–63, as well as *TDP* 15, 45, 137–38; *BPWS* 67, 73–74, 106, 178; *PIE* 87–89; *PIA* 86; *OHF* 12, 35–37; *BCAP* 12, 141–42, 229.

[59] See *SZ* 152–53, 393–95; *BCAP* 187; *HCT* 20, as well as *TDP* 25–26, 45, 64–69, 154–55; *BPWS* 40–41, 72–75, 113, 118, 155, 160, 163, 175; *PIE* 9, 118–19; and *OHF* 43–45, 53–57.

[60] Singham (2021) offers an accessible account of this episode.

[61] My account follows Keller's well-known treatment (1983, Chapters 8–12).

[62] See Fedoroff (2012, esp. p. 20201).

3.2.3 Physicalism Distorts Our Understanding of Science

Heidegger thinks that physicalism distorts our understanding science by emphasizing propositional truth over the more relevant disclosed truth.[63] This view comes out especially in an extended discussion of Descartes and the birth of mathematical physics in *IPR* 156–73.[64] For Descartes, Heidegger writes,

> [t]he objects [of science] must be such that, insofar as they are comprehended, they can yield nothing uncertain . . .. [T]hey must be purum et simplex [pure and simple] . . .. For the simpler the objects, the less danger that something obscure remains in the comprehension of them. The idea of the science prefigures the basic constitution of its possible objects. The disciplines that yield objects of this sort are arithmetic and geometry. It is apparent from this that Descartes has oriented his idea of science and scientific knowing to the fact of the matter of mathematical disciplines[.] . . . Not only is the *idea of the possible objects of science* prefigured from the standpoint of mathematics, but at the same time the *idea of method* is acquired in a definite radicalization[.] (*IPR* 161)

Mathematical judgments are uniquely apodictic. For empirical claims, further information is always relevant, so the course of history can reveal any erstwhile "truth" to be false. But mathematics, because its objects are maximally "pure and simple" (that is, nonempirical and clearly definable), yields *theorems*. Our judgments about its statements' truth values are uniquely conclusive. If we accept MP or PES, then physics' achievement – successfully mathematizing nature – ultimately sets the standard for the other sciences. The ideal is to develop theories that apply to empirical phenomena – Descartes ultimately recommends a thoroughly geometrical treatment of natural phenomena[65] – but are as secure as those of mathematics. Reasoning via formal, quantitative propositions, which yields maximally certain conclusions, becomes the canonical form of scientific thinking and the aspect of science thought to constitute its epistemic merit.

In this way, MP and PES contribute to a significant problem in the philosophy of science: the failure to appreciate disclosed truth. This is not a problem, Heidegger thinks, for scientists (including physicists) themselves, whose bread and butter is uncovering and disclosure.[66] But Heidegger thinks that physicalism tempts philosophers into believing that science's primary aim is *theory construction* in the sense of identifying a set of propositions that can be securely judged to be true *à la* mathematics.

---

[63] See Section 2.2.   [64] See also *SZ* 96–97 and *SZ* §§33, 69b.

[65] *IPR* 169; see also notes 85 and 86, as well as the extended discussion of Descartes in Section 3.3.

[66] See note 6.

> Science in general may be defined as the totality established through an interconnection of true propositions. This definition is not complete, nor does it reach the meaning of science. (*SZ* 11)[67]

Heidegger calls this a "logical" approach to the philosophy science (*SZ* 10, 357), which understands science as the pursuit of propositional truth. Heidegger (as is too often his wont) does not specify his targets. Presumably, he has in mind Husserl and the Neo-Kantians.[68] But figures more familiar in Anglophone philosophy of science, such as Wittgenstein, Carnap, Popper, Hempel, and Quine, also arguably fit this description at various points in their careers.[69] Note that the "logical approach" he criticizes is a version of SCS, which holds that science primarily seeks to develop increasingly comprehensive, successful – and thus secure – theories; the "logical approach" claims that science aims to identify a maximally complete, coherent, and secure set of propositions.

Heidegger dubs his alternative an *existential* approach to philosophy of science, which "understands science as a way of existence and thus as a mode of being-in-the-world, which uncovers or discloses either entities or being" (*SZ* 357). In other words, science is to be investigated as a uniquely *disclosive* kind of pursuit rather than as a set of theoretical results:

> [S]cience should never be equated with its results, results that are then passed from hand to hand . . . . [S]cience never makes itself known as science in its results. [W]hat is essential to science [lies] . . . rather in that which is appropriated ever anew. (GA27 32)

For Heidegger, disclosed truth is more relevant to science than propositional truth: science opens up access to (i.e., "appropriates anew") its subject matter. Developing rigorous theories happens to be one important activity of science. But there are many others: identifying overlooked phenomena; developing effective examples, analogies, thought experiments, and arguments that point out particular features of interest or illustrate how a given phenomenon should be understood; manipulating an array of specialized equipment to allow a given phenomenon to show itself clearly; and so on. The common aim of these activities is not to develop an ever more

---

[67] See also *IPR* 2.

[68] See, e.g., *HCT* 17. In a similar discussion in GA27 (pp. 48ff.), Heidegger names Husserl and Hermann Cohen as targets. And in an early version of this critique in *IPR*, Heidegger claims that Husserl – and indeed, the whole modern philosophical tradition – fetishizes what he calls "already known knowledge" (see pp. 43ff.). See also Husserl (2001, p. 18), Cassirer (2015), Natorp (2015a), and Natorp (2015b).

[69] See Wittgenstein (1981, p. 75), Carnap (2011), Popper (2002), Hempel (1965, pp. 331–496), and Quine (2013, pp. 207–13).

comprehensive, successful set of theories, but rather, to open up access to some unseen, unappreciated, or forgotten piece of reality – i.e., to uncover entities and their features (e.g., the discovery and skeletal reconstruction of our distant ancestor Lucy) or, more fundamentally, to disclose the being of a given subject matter (e.g., the articulation of what it means to be a distant human ancestor).[70]

Heidegger's existential approach to science thus advances ACS, whereas physicalism promotes SCS, which Heidegger sees as impoverished.

3.2.4 Physicalism Is a Consequence of Historical Falling

Heidegger offers a genealogical argument in *SZ* that constitutes an indirect objection to physicalism, similar to how Nietzsche's *Genealogy* advances an indirect objection of Christian morality.[71] This argument, in other words, does not establish that physicalism is false but rather that it emerges as the result of an epistemically suspect process. Heidegger's genealogy also addresses a looming question: given that he thinks physicalism is misguided, Heidegger owes us an explanation of its currency.

Heidegger's genealogy depends on a concept that is essential to Heidegger's work, which I call *historical falling*. Historical falling is the tendency for communities, rather than individuals, passively to accept the prevailing norms of intelligibility – i.e., the commonsense views of what is real or illusory, fundamental or peripheral, valuable or trivial, and so on.[72] Heidegger discusses it at length in *SZ*:

> *Dasein* . . . falls with respect to [*verfällt in*] the tradition which it has more or less explicitly grasped [*ergriffenen*]. This tradition keeps it from providing its own guidance, whether in inquiring or in choosing . . . .
>
> When tradition becomes master, it does so in such a way that what it 'transmits' is made so inaccessible . . . that it rather becomes concealed. Tradition takes what has come down to us and delivers it over to self-evidence; it blocks our access to those primordial 'sources' from which the categories and concepts handed down to us have been in part quite genuinely drawn. Indeed it makes us forget that they have such an origin, and makes us suppose that the necessity of going back to these sources is something which we need not even understand. (21)

What originally was a confrontational discovery or innovation eventually declines to become a mundane aspect of the everyday (e.g., we now accept heliocentrism as a matter of course). Historical falling occurs cyclically

[70] See *IPR* 2, 55; *BCAP* 12, 29, 71; and *HCT* 3. On "reality," see note 1.
[71] Nietzsche (1969), First Essay.   [72] On falling, see Section 2.3.

because, as with falling in general, resolute intellectual decisions – i.e., ground-breaking disclosures – are fragile and subject to eventual dissolution.

Heidegger thinks, therefore, that we must occasionally renew our access to the original sense of our ossified concepts and beliefs. This renewal, which Heidegger calls *destruction* (*Destruktion*), happens when we undertake a historical analysis that unearths the grounding experiences out of which our concepts and beliefs emerged.[73]

For Heidegger, physicalism is a result of historical falling. It is premised on a dogmatic metaphysical commitment from the ancient Greeks that privileges entities with a specific temporal orientation – stability, or being completely and unvaryingly present. But whereas the Greeks acknowledge this commitment (and thus understand some of its limitations), modern thinkers (above all Descartes) dogmatically assume it and thus set the stage for physicalism. Heidegger wants to make us aware of our tacit commitment, the better to recognize and transcend its limitations. This metaphysical commitment is ultimately motivated, he contends, by an irrational evasion of existential anxiety and uncanniness. I now develop these claims.

3.3 What Is Physicalism's Historical Origin?

Motion, in the broad sense of flux, is a central theme of ancient Greek philosophy. Everything on Earth is temporary, subject to change and contingency. Things grow, decay, and die; they are subject to exhaustion, destruction, and transformation. In other words, earthly things are dynamic and structurally incomplete; as Aristotle suggests in his discussion of *eudaimonia* and fortune, our lives are incomplete until we die – and death does not "complete" us so much as it destroys us.[74] Thus, at any given moment, earthly things offer only a limited slice of themselves. (For instance, a butterfly is never simultaneously all of its life stages.) The decisive ancient Greek thinkers – Heidegger names Aristotle, Plato, and Parmenides in *SZ* 25–26 – all find this earthly realm of flux ontologically deficient. The true or supreme reality as they conceive it – the unmoved mover and the heavenly bodies (Aristotle), the forms (Plato), being (Parmenides) – is maximally stable; more precisely, it is complete, immutable, and eternal. The most real things lack nothing proper to them at any moment.

Take Aristotle on the heavenly bodies.[75] To the naked eye, the heavens exhibit profound regularity; Babylonian astronomical records stretching back centuries were available to the Greeks, and they confirmed that the heavenly bodies move in apparently unchanging cycles.[76] The heavens appear to be both

---

[73] See *SZ* 22–23, *BPP* 22–23.   [74] *Nicomachean Ethics* 1.10–1.11, 1099b9-1101b9.
[75] See also Plato, *Timaeus*, 37c-40b, 47a-c, 90a-d.   [76] Clarke (1962, p. 70).

active yet curiously immune to the pervasive exhaustion, decay, and destruction on Earth.[77] Aristotle's bifurcated concept of locomotion, which Heidegger unpacks in his 1935 *QT* (pp. 56-60), drives this point home.[78] Heavenly bodies move *rotationally* while earthly bodies move *rectilinearly*. Notice, however, that the end (*telos*) of rectilinear motion brings motion to a halt. Nothing on Earth, then, both moves and achieves its end; the one forecloses the other. But rotational motion is different: its end is radial distance from the origin. Thus, a rotating thing achieves its end at every point along its path. Earthly motion is imperfect while heavenly motion is perfect. (See Figure 1.)

The heavenly bodies are thus most real because they are completely and eternally present – they are not only immortal but also perfectly active. Things on Earth (including humans) are ontologically deficient because they are incomplete and temporally dispersed; a residue of potentiality always inheres. Heidegger thus writes the following about the Greeks:

> [T]hat which *only* maintains itself in being-completed, such that it is *what excludes every dunamis*; a completed being that is there, which is *always already completed*, which was never produced, which never would be but is *simply present*. That which excludes the possibility of having not been also excludes the possibility of ever *disappearing*. The present of such a being is not thought up, but is seen in the movement of the heavens[.] (*BCAP* 201; see also p. 196)

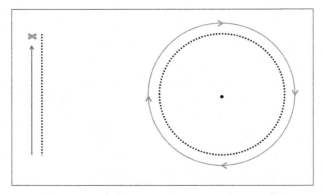

Figure 1 Visualizing imperfect rectilinear earthly motion (left) and perfect rotational heavenly motion (right).

---

[77] Aristotle, *On the Heavens* 1.3, 270b1-270b31 and 2.1, 284a21-284b6; Aristotle, *Metaphysics* 9.8, 1050b18-28.

[78] Aristotle, *Physics* 8.9, 265a12-266a9; *On the Heavens* 2.6, 288a12-289a12.

> For the Greeks, to be means to be present; and what is or had being in the proper sense is that which is always present and never is not. Thus, the highest manner of being consists simply in the purest and simplest presence. However, this implies that the entity that is in this way [the heavenly bodies] never was not, but always already was *and* always already was the way it now is present, finished and complete. (*BH* 225)[79]

Heidegger thinks these ontological commitments have seismic ramifications. The heavenly bodies' exemplary stability (presence and completeness) for the Greeks inaugurates the dominance of the ontological notion that Heidegger calls "presence-at-hand" in *SZ*: subsequently, in Western metaphysics, to be means to be "present" or "on-hand," such that *maximally* present entities are considered most real.

Heidegger observes that Aristotle extends metaphysical concepts suited to one particular kind (the heavenly bodies) to other domains – e.g., consider his analysis of the *bios theoretikos* as divine, or his claim that organisms reproduce to approximate heavenly immortality.[80] Heidegger's worry is that Dasein has been analyzed with the aid of inappropriate ontological concepts (presence, completeness, presence-at-hand):

> Greek ontology and its history . . . prove that when Dasein understands either itself or being in general, it does so in terms of the 'world' [i.e., "the totality of those entities which can be present-at-hand within the world" (*SZ* 64–65)] and that the ontology which has thus arisen has fallen with respect to [*verfällt*] a tradition in which it gets reduced to something self-evident[.] (*SZ* 21–22)

His remark about the "tradition" is striking. His claim, I believe, is that the Greeks mitigate his worry because they are aware that their ontological scheme privileges the heavenly bodies and only partially illuminates imperfect earthly things. For instance, Aristotle recognizes the need to problematize the phenomenon of imperfect motion.[81] And most of the *Nicomachean Ethics* examines the virtues relevant to dynamic social life, such as *phronesis*. (Indeed, despite claiming that the *bios theoretikos* is the supreme human life, Aristotle suggests that the *bios politikos* is the distinctively human life.[82]) Crucially, however, the tradition degenerates as its commitment to Greek metaphysics becomes increasingly dogmatic.

Medieval theologians, Heidegger thinks, also rely on Greek metaphysics. Now God, the cosmos' creator and superintendent, is ontologically supreme – but on the same grounds that, for the Greeks, rendered the heavenly bodies

---

[79] See also *PS* 122, 323–24; *SZ* 21–22, 25–26.
[80] See note 12. On reproduction, see Aristotle, *On the Soul* 2.4, 415a25-415b9.
[81] See *Physics* 3.1–3.3, 200b10-202b29.
[82] *Nicomachean Ethics* 10.7–10.8, 1177a11-1178b34. Plato's *Republic* (Book 7, 517a-521d) evinces a similar ambivalence.

ontologically supreme: God is maximally complete (God is perfect, and hence, lacks nothing) and present (God is omnipresent, immutable, and eternal).[83]

Similarly, in an extended discussion in *SZ* §§19–22, Heidegger argues that modern thinkers, for all their innovations, maintain an especially dogmatic commitment to ancient Greek metaphysics, a key result of which is physicalism. Interestingly, Heidegger thinks that Descartes, despite not being committed to OP himself—famously, he believes that the mind is irreducible to the body—is the paradigmatic figure. Descartes' ontology privileges different kinds of entities – minds (*res cogitans*) and bodies (*res extensa*).[84] But his rationale betrays his reliance on Greek metaphysical assumptions: these things are maximally stable; they best approximate perfect, unvarying presence-at-hand. For Heidegger, Descartes's treatment of bodies, which I unpack below, articulates key assumptions that allow physicalism to emerge.

Descartes thinks the basic characteristic of external objects (i.e., entities that we perceive in the world and in nature) – is extension in length, width, and depth.[85] He justifies this claim as follows: every other feature (e.g., color, texture, weight, hardness) asymmetrically depends on spatial extension. As such, when we strip all other features, an extended body still remains; but when we strip the thing's spatial extension, all its other features are thereby destroyed. Spatial extension is thus external entities' one feature that cannot be removed without destroying them. For instance, take a stone. If we remove all its features other than spatial extension, we still have an external object. Meanwhile, if we remove the stone's spatial extension, we have entirely destroyed it. Therefore, the stone essentially *is* its spatial extension. Descartes' physics thus aims to reduce all other features to variations of geometrical extension and motion.

But Descartes' argument tacitly presupposes Greek metaphysics. Spatial extension may indeed be necessary condition for being an external object. But this fact does not prove that extension is the essence of all external objects. It only could be taken for such proof if we conceive of being as complete presence. To illustrate, consider an alternative interpretation of the example. Perhaps when we remove the stone's texture, hardness, color (and so on) we are in fact destroying one entity (the stone) and what remains is a different entity (a merely extended body). On this alternative view, the set of all external objects is much wider than the set of all merely extended bodies. Just as a statue is not

---

[83] *SZ* 21–25, 93; see also *IPR* 120–47 and GA23, pp. 41–103.

[84] I am oversimplifying; Descartes claims that God is ontologically supreme. But within the realm of creation, the *res cogitans* and *res extensa* are ontologically supreme. See Heidegger's helpful and concise discussion on *SZ* 92.

[85] My remarks here and later are based on *Principles of Philosophy* (Descartes 1983), Part I, §§53, 69–70 and Part II, §§1, 3–4, 10–11, 64.

identical to its matter, so too external entities are not identical to their spatial extension. Descartes' argument thus shows that spatial extension is the most *present* (stable, persisting) feature of external objects, not that it is the *essence* of external objects as such.

Descartes' commitment to Greek metaphysics also can be gleaned from his geometrical approach to nature. His methodological writings explicitly model proper reasoning on mathematical reasoning.[86] Mathematics uniquely furnishes us with certain knowledge. And it is able to do so, Heidegger claims, because mathematical objects (shapes, numbers, operators, variables, etc.) are accessible yet – unlike empirical objects – paradigmatically eternal, not subject to decay or change.[87] The properties of a triangle are the same now as they ever were or will be.

In other words, mathematical objects are exemplars of complete presence. Things like organisms, and even rocks, are intrinsically dynamic and hence incomplete, but numbers, equations, and geometrical relationships are wholly present at every moment. We thus can attain certainty in mathematics because we can be assured that, blunders notwithstanding, we have completely grasped our subject matter. History won't reveal anything that will render our conclusions false.

Thus, Descartes mathematizes nature because he seeks empirical knowledge that approximates the certainty we can achieve about mathematical objects. And he fetishizes certainty because he is dogmatically committed to the Greeks' presence-at-hand–privileging metaphysics. Heidegger expresses his interpretation with remarkable clarity in one passage:

> Mathematical knowledge is regarded by Descartes as the one manner of apprehending entities which can always give assurance that their being has been securely grasped. If anything measures up in its own kind of being to the being that is accessible in mathematical knowledge, then it *is* in the authentic sense. Such entities are those *which always are what they are* . . .. That which enduringly remains really *is* . . .. Thus the being of the 'world' is, as it were, dictated to it in terms of a definite idea of being which lies veiled in the concept of substantiality . . .. [Descartes] prescribes for the world its 'real' being, as it were, on the basis of an idea of being whose source has not been unveiled and which has not been demonstrated in its own right – an idea in which being is equated with constant presence-at-hand. Thus his ontology of the world is not primarily determined by his leaning towards mathematics, a science which he chances to esteem very highly, but rather by his

---

ontological orientation in principle towards being as constant presence-at-hand, which mathematical knowledge is exceptionally well suited to grasp.

The Greeks understand that their metaphysics privileges certain entities and fails to illuminate the flux that is apparent in everyday earthly phenomena. But Descartes adopts Greek metaphysics uncritically; in doing so, he sets the stage for physicalism. Heidegger continues:

> In this way Descartes explicitly carries out [*vollzieht*] the shift [*Umschaltung*] philosophically from the development of traditional ontology to modern mathematical physics and its transcendental foundations. (*SZ* 95–96)[88]

The most enduring mathematizable things of nature, those to which we can reduce all others, are what truly exist. And the mathematical sciences set the standard of rigor. Although Descartes' physics lost out to Newton's, Descartes nonetheless lays out the philosophical parameters for physicalism and, concomitantly, SCS. Science aims to produce theories that approach the form and certainty of mathematical proofs – phrased in maximally precise, unambiguous, and ideally quantitative expressions; and organized in logically perspicuous, deductive relationships. And the regulative ideal of science is reduction to elementary quantitative physics (much as geometrical truths are reducible to their axioms). Thus, any subject matter that resists reduction appears suspect.

Heidegger suspects that Greek metaphysics – and, *a fortiori*, physicalism – are motivated by an evasion of existential anxiety and Dasein's uncanniness.[89]

> [T]hat in the face of which existence *flees* by way of the *care about certainty*, is an *uncanniness* [*Unheimlichkeit*]. Uncanniness is the genuine threat that existence is subject to. (*IPR* 221)

Recall that our existence is uncanny because although the public has always decided on a particular interpretation of reality, it is in fact radically open. Anxiety discloses this uncanniness. Our own existence is dynamic, structurally incomplete, and threatened constantly with dissolution; hence, our grasp on reality is neither complete nor certain. Furthermore, most things that we experience are dynamic; mathematical objects (or the heavenly bodies for the Greeks, or God for the medievals) are some of the few exceptions. We constantly discover novelty or error that forces us to refine our concepts. Fetishizing certainty, and reducing reality to what is ascertainable – to what is complete, immutable, and accessible to us – allows us to evade everything else. Most importantly, Heidegger postulates, these epistemological and metaphysical

---

[88] See also *HCT* 184–85, *BH* 231.
[89] See *IPR* 70–71, 213–21, 240–42; *BCAP* 129, 196–97, 201.

commitments, which undergird physicalism, allow us to evade the anxious-making facts of our own finite, incomplete existence.

But what is Heidegger's proposed alternative to physicalism and SCS? I turn now to this question.

4 The Early Heidegger on Science, Truth, and Authenticity

While discussing physics, Heidegger makes a telling remark in passing:

> This awaiting of uncoveredness [*Entdecktheit*] has its ... basis in a resoluteness by which Dasein projects itself toward its ability-to-be [*Seinkönnen*] in the 'truth'. This projection is possible because being-in-the-truth makes up a definite way in which Dasein may exist. We shall not trace further how science has its origin [*Ursprung*] in authentic existence. (*SZ* 363)

Below, I unpack this brief but suggestive hint about Heidegger's positive approach to science via ACS.[90] What is the relationship between science, "being-in-the-truth," and authenticity? I discuss science and truth (4.1) before turning to authenticity (4.2) and offering some brief concluding remarks (4.3).

4.1 Science and Truth

Recall the distinction between SCS and ACS. The former, which Heidegger rejects, privileges propositional truth: it views science's primary aim as formulating maximally secure theories. The latter, which Heidegger advances, privileges disclosed truth and views science's primary aim as opening up access to reality, acquainting (or re-acquainting) us with things and what it means to be a given kind of thing.

But it's worth noting that opening up access to reality is not unique to science. Skills like cooking are disclosive: a good cook uncovers features of food and kitchen equipment (e.g., peeling, chopping, salting, and roasting sweet potatoes on high heat brings out their sweetness, resiliency, and tenderness). Art is also disclosive; the later Heidegger famously describes how a van Gogh painting discloses what it means to be a trusty pair of shoes and how a Greek temple brings out the beauty and terror of nature.[91] So what is unique to scientific disclosure?

Heidegger's answer can be found in his scattershot analysis of the notions of *thematizing*, *projection*, and *objectivity* (*Objektivität*).[92] The first and third

---

[90] See also GA27 211. Beck (2005) and Haugeland (2013, pp. 187–220, especially pp. 214–17) offer alternative interpretations of this *SZ* remark.

[91] *OBT* 13–16, 20–22.

[92] See also Heidegger's related discussion of *objektivieren* in *SZ* 363 and *Vergegenständlichung* in *BPP* 281–82, 320–30.

concepts are described only briefly, so I will have to extrapolate. Nevertheless, Heidegger provides the germs of an illuminating analysis.

By *thematizing*, Heidegger means that scientific disclosure is discursive, conceptual, and systematic.

> Every science is constituted primarily by thematizing. That which is familiar pre-scientifically in Dasein as disclosed being-in-the-world, gets projected upon the being which is specific to it. With this projection, the realm of entities is bounded off. The ways of access to them get 'managed' methodologically, and the conceptual structure for interpreting them is outlined. (*SZ* 393; see also *SZ* 363)

Cooks disclose primarily by preparing and presenting their dishes for consumption. Novelists and poets produce works that are, to some degree, conceptual and discursive. But they generally do not prioritize systematicity. The scientist, however, develops and works within a set of systematic *basic concepts* that comprises a given discipline's ontological, epistemological, and methodological principles.

> When the basic concepts of that understanding of being by which we are guided have been worked out, the clues of its methods, the structure of its way of conceiving things, the possibility of truth and certainty which belongs to it, the ways in which things get grounded or proved, the mode in which it is binding for us, and the way it is communicated – all these will be determined. (*SZ* 362–63[93])

Take, for instance, motion: all of us have a pre-theoretical acquaintance with motion. But Aristotelian and Newtonian physics analyze motion via a set of foundational, systematic concepts.

Aristotle thematizes flux, and so movement across space (*loco*motion) is merely a species of motion (motion also comprises, e.g., growth, decay, transformation, and destruction).[94] Aristotle further analyzes locomotion: heavy objects move downward because their dominant elements are earth or water, which naturally strive toward the center of the Earth; light objects move upward because their dominant elements are air or fire, which naturally strive toward the heavens. Meanwhile, heavenly bodies are composed of aether, which naturally moves rotationally. Natural objects thus have their respective *proper places*: specified domains wherein they reside or toward which they move.[95]

Classical physics, by contrast, does not conceive of locomotion as a species of a more general phenomenon of change; it reduces rotational motion to

---

[93] See also *SZ* 9–10.   [94] *Physics* 3.1, 200b10-201b15, and 8.7, 260a20-261b26.
[95] *Physics* 8.4, 254b7-256a3; *On the Heavens* 1.2–1.3, 268b10-270b31. See Heidegger's comments on *PS* 69–83.

rectilinear motion with the help of concepts like inertia, gravity, and friction. Thus, circular motion, as Heidegger writes in his later *QT* lectures, "is now no longer the grounding basis," i.e., the paradigm of perfect motion.[96] Now, it is "precisely what needs grounding" (*QT* 59) – i.e., it must be explained as an apparent deviation from inertial, rectilinear motion. Relatedly, Heidegger points out that absent Aristotle's differentiation between different basic kinds (and correspondingly different ends) of motion, the notion of *proper places* drops out of classical physics in favor of arbitrary spatial position (*QT* 59).

So much for thematizing. But our discussion has tacitly presupposed the concept of projection. Thematizing involves the development of a set of basic concepts. Projection concerns how these basic concepts are used to structure subsequent research. We encountered this concept in Section 2.1; recall that projections orient us by pre-structuring our engagement with things in accordance with some future possibility, such that we attend to things salient to that possibility and ignore the rest. Scientific disclosures are themselves *projectival*: research is pre-structured by the thematic basic concepts.[97]

Let's return to Aristotle and Newton. Given Aristotle's broad concept of motion, his physics is qualitative rather than quantitative: calculating rates of motion is relatively uninteresting; more interesting is identifying the kinds of motion proper to a given thing. Conversely, Newtonian physics is quantitative instead of qualitative in part because of Newton's narrow concept of motion as rectilinear locomotion; on this view, defining rates, trajectories, and influences on locomotion becomes the chief way to analyze and differentiate moving things.

Note that Heidegger's notion of scientific projection anticipates Kuhn: the scientist is distinguished not by her empirical openness (first approximating a *tabula rasa* and proceeding inductively) but, instead, by her acceptance of rigid constraints. What appears salient or trivial – as a puzzle to be solved, a problem to be shelved, or a distraction to be sidestepped – is pre-figured or "projected" by the scientist's thematic disclosure.

So much for projection. We now come to objectivity. Heidegger's analysis here is underdeveloped, but one comment is especially suggestive:

> [T]he objectivity of a science is regulated primarily in terms of whether that science can *confront* [*entgegenbringen*] us with the entity which belongs to it as its theme, and can *bring* [*entgegenbringen*] it, uncovered in the primordiality of its being, to our understanding. (*SZ* 395; emphasis Heidegger's)

---

[96] See Figure 1 and Section 3.3.   [97] See *SZ* 362–63, *HCCR* 32–33.

His point, let me suggest, is that science is committed to demonstrability, i.e., to making the portion of reality it thematizes accessible and responsive to public scrutiny. My reading particularly relies on the italicized verb *entgegenbringen*, rendered with two words ("confront" and "bring") to capture its full sense. *Entgegenbringen* means, literally, "to bring out into relief"; colloquially, "to show," "to meet with," "to demonstrate" – e.g., "he showed respect," "she met the proposal with great interest." Science's virtue, Heidegger suggests, lies in its ethic of demonstrability rather than in its alleged adherence to a common method.

Heideggerian objectivity, on my reading, bears a striking resemblance to Helen Longino's concept of objectivity. Longino argues that objectivity has little to do with individual researchers' disinterest (emotional detachment, absence of bias). Instead, Longinoan objectivity applies to science as a social enterprise: a science is objective, roughly, to the degree that it is open and responsive to public criticism.[98] Similarly, for Heidegger, science is objective not because sound scientific reasoning adheres to some privileged logical schema(s). Rather, science is objective insofar as it makes its thematized objects accessible to a concrete audience.

Science, for Heidegger, thus discloses and uncovers via research that is projectival, thematic, and objective – i.e., pre-structured in accordance with a set of basic concepts and guided by a norm of demonstrability to a concrete audience. But my discussion so far has been fairly abstract. What are some concrete consequences for philosophers and scientists?

1. Heidegger undermines the significance of the distinction between the "context of discovery" and the "context of justification" in science, by which some philosophers (especially in the early and middle twentieth century) set great store. The former concerns how scientists in fact discover and formulate their ideas, concepts, claims, and so on; the latter concerns how scientists' claims and theories can be tested and justified, especially whether and how they pass muster when rationally reconstructed. Philosophers, the thought goes, should focus on the context of justification and leave the context of discovery to psychologists, sociologists, and other empirical scientists.[99] Heidegger would see this distinction as emerging out of the misguided SCS.[100] Approaching science primarily by rationally reconstructing scientific theories is a consequence of thinking that science's primary

---

[98] Longino (1990, pp. 62–79).

[99] See Reichenbach (1938, pp. 5–7, 381–82), Hempel (1966, pp. 15–18), and Popper (2002, pp. 7–9). I must pass over important nuances and differences in how philosophers articulate this distinction and its significance.

[100] Feyerabend (1993, pp. 148–49) offers another objection to this distinction's significance; (see also Kuhn 2012, Chapter 1; Longino 1990, Chapter 4; and Kitcher 2011, Chapter 1, Section 4). For commentary on Heidegger in a similar vein, see Kisiel (1977, pp. 166–67).

aim is to establish secure claims and theories. But if we accept ACS, on which science primarily aims to open up access to reality, which occurs historically and always to a concrete audience, then it's clear that philosophers should not pass over the context of discovery if they want to understand what is essential to science (and indeed, what accounts for its epistemic virtue).[101]

2. Current scientific norms almost exclusively support research on esoteric puzzles. I suspect that Heideggerian science would differ by granting significant resources and prestige to effective popular presentations of science.[102] To be clear, esoteric research would still be a priority; it stands on the frontiers of knowledge and hence opens up access to hitherto concealed regions of reality. But effective accounts of science aimed at the general public are also disclosive and objective in Heidegger's sense: they make the thematized objects of research accessible to the educated public. If only a handful of specialists are able to understand research, then science has in an important respect failed to make good on its ethic of demonstrability. Thus, those with the unique skills to identify and articulate a field's key insights for the general public are bona fide Heideggerian scientists.

3. Perhaps the chief consequence of Heideggerian science, for scientists and philosophers alike, is the embrace of science's dynamic character and, in particular, of scientific crises.[103] Several passages are worth quoting at length.

> [C]risis is not to be overcome, but to become vital ... so that the sciences in general may come to exist in the way that they want to in accordance with their essence. (GA27 39)

> [In crises], [t]he basic relationship to the subject matters is becoming insecure, which activates the tendency to carry out a propaedeutic reflection on their basic structure .... Genuine progress in the sciences occurs only in this field of reflection. Such crises do not take place in the historical [*historischen*] sciences only because they have not yet reached the degree of maturity necessary for revolutions.
>
> The present crisis in all the sciences therefore stems from the burgeoning tendency in them to reclaim their particular domain of objects originally, to

---

[101] See also the penultimate paragraph of Section 3.2.3 for relevant remarks.

[102] Heidegger inveighs against popularizations of science in GA27 (pp. 29ff., 40). But there he appears to connect "popularizations" with SCS, which he rejects. If we understand "popularizations" in a broader sense – as communicating not primarily the settled results of scientific research, but rather its motivations, problems, and historical developments – they are perfectly consistent with ACS.

[103] Beck (2005, pp. 164–68) and Rouse (2005, pp. 175–80) make similar points.

forge their way back to the field of subject matter which is thematizable in their research.

... [T]he exposition of the primary field of subject matter calls for a mode of experience and interpretation in principle different from those which prevail in the concrete sciences themselves. In crisis, scientific research assumes a philosophical cast. (*HCT* 3)

[Science's] real progress comes not so much from collecting results and storing them away in 'manuals' as from inquiring into the ways in which each particular area is basically constituted – an inquiry to which we have been driven mostly by reacting against just such an increase in information.

The real 'movement' of the sciences takes place when their basic concepts undergo a more or less radical revision which is transparent to itself. The level which a science has reached is determined by how far it is *capable* of a crisis in its basic concepts. In such immanent crises the very relationship between positively investigative inquiry and those things themselves that are under interrogation comes to a point where it begins to totter. (*SZ* 9)

Heidegger's account is sketchy but anticipates some insights from Kuhn – above all, that science develops in biphasic cycles consisting of a revolutionary crisis phase and a positivistic consolidation phase (which correspond to Kuhn's "extraordinary science" and "normal science"). Moreover, like Kuhn, Heidegger claims that crises are spurred, paradoxically, as a science reaches "maturity" in its positivistic consolidation phase. Heidegger is sketchy on what constitutes maturity, but he suggests that a mature sciences has a well-defined set of basic concepts (*SZ* 362–63) and has accumulated a hefty amount of positive "information" (*SZ* 9) about its subject matter.

Note, however, a key difference in Heidegger's and Kuhn's respective evaluations of science's epistemic merit. Kuhn stops short of making any prescriptions; nevertheless, he makes clear that nearly all the goods we associate with modern science (above all, increasingly esoteric knowledge that enables technological development) flow from normal science (2012, pp. 17–25), which crises interrupt by directing inquiry back to foundational issues. Heidegger, meanwhile, views crises favorably *because* they direct inquiry back to foundational philosophical issues. Foundational inquiry leads researchers to renew their access to reality by disclosing unseen, forgotten, or underappreciated domains of reality.[104] By contrast, "normal" phases lead inexorably to the ossifying consensus that we discussed earlier as "historical falling."[105]

---

[104] In addition to the passages quoted earlier, see *BCAP* 12, 71, 74–75, 188–90, 192, 243.
[105] See Section 3.2.4.

The last two sentences underscore Heidegger's existential approach to science. Kuhn explains science's biphasic cycles purely in terms of research problems that scientists confront – namely, successful paradigms lead to esoteric research, which tends to generate recognized anomalies, which, over time, engender crises out of which a new paradigm emerges. But Heidegger also suggests an existential explanation for science's biphasic cycles: science is a pursuit of Dasein's; and Dasein, as we saw earlier, moves through biphasic cycles of achieving authenticity via resolute decisions and subsequently falling into inauthenticity.

4.2 Science and Authenticity

We have just seen that Heidegger is committed to the following two claims.

1. Science is the pursuit of disclosed truth (i.e., science essentially opens up access to reality via thematic, projectival, and objective research).
2. Scientific research occurs in biphasic cycles, with a revolutionary crisis phase spurring a positivistic consolidation phase, which eventually engenders a new crisis, and so on.

I also identified a parallel between science's biphasic cycle (crisis-consolidation) and Dasein's biphasic cycle (authenticity-inauthenticity), which recalls Heidegger's remark quoted at the start of Section 4. I thus read Heidegger as committed to a third claim:.

3. The disclosures that occasion and resolve scientific crises require authenticity; crises demand researchers who are resolute in the face of uncanniness and death.

Before I unpack this claim, let me note an important caveat: Heidegger fails to detail how scientific disclosures relate to his analysis of authenticity. The account I offer next is therefore schematic and speculative, and I rely on Kuhn to flesh out some of Heidegger's suggestions.[106]

The aspiring scientist learns the prevailing norms of intelligibility for their community – above all, an established set of basic concepts that delineates a working ontology and methodology for their subject matter, but also, a sense of the past achievements in their field and of the day's more or less pressing problems.[107] And Kuhn famously writes that normal science generally does not aim "to produce major novelties, conceptual or phenomenal" (2012, p. 35);

---

[106] Haugeland (2013, pp. 187–220) offers an alternative reading of this same issue.

[107] This sense of "norms" corresponds roughly to the "disciplinary matrix" sense of paradigms in Kuhn (2012, pp. 181–86).

rather, it consists of "mop-up work" – often requiring profound ingenuity – of roughly three kinds: "determination of significant fact, matching of facts with theory, and articulation of theory" (2012, pp. 24, 34). We might thus understand Heidegger's suggestion that the scientist's everyday research is generally inauthentic. The scientist is trained to accept passively the authority of the prevailing norms – i.e., to measure their actions against such norms, and hence, to view themselves third-personally as *one* engaged in their research program: research generally aims to refine established models or to assimilate recalcitrant phenomena ("anomalies") to them. This account helps us understand a remark that otherwise appears obtuse and disparaging: "the scientific work of one individual," Heidegger writes, "can in principle always be represented by someone else; the scientific discoveries that one person makes could also have been made by someone else" (GA27 225–26). The researcher in positivistic consolidation phases, Heidegger suggests, evades self-ownership by passing off responsibility to the prevailing norms.[108]

Crises call the reigning norms into question; they are ultimately resolved (though they also may be occasioned or exacerbated) by scientists who venture a new disclosure and, in so doing, achieve authenticity. To disclose reality anew requires an antecedent recognition that the norms of intelligibility – and with them, one's identity as a scientist – are fragile, subject to contingency, change, and dissolution (existential death). This recognition leads to the breakdown in the world's apparent coherence that is constitutive of anxiety and uncanniness. Indeed, Kuhn claims that crises are utterly disorienting, both theoretically and personally. The world that previously seemed well understood now appears "out of joint" and disturbingly open (2012, p. 79). The scientist must face her inalienable responsibility to interpret reality; the veneer of authority the norms previously had disintegrates. Their contingency, fragility, and generic nature – i.e., the fact that they underdetermine the scientist's research in any concrete situation – is now palpable. Facing this responsibility shakes the scientist out of their prior falling. They are brought into the concrete situation; i.e., they attend to their subject matter with fresh eyes rather than passively understanding them via staid, generic norms. Indeed, Kuhn writes that crises generally involve the "loosening of the rules for normal research" (2012, p. 84). The scientist can thus discover latent possibilities for research, and, in so doing, venture a creative "reply" to their tradition, which yields a new ontological

---

[108] Heidegger generally suggests that researchers in positivistic consolidation (or "normal") phases are inauthentic; (e.g., *BPP* 54). Occasionally, however, he seems ambivalent – see, e.g., *P* 83 and *IM* 48. This ambivalence deserves a treatment of its own; I suspect that it is related to ambiguities in Heidegger's concepts of falling and authenticity that Dreyfus (1991, pp. 225–26, 313–15) and Carman (2005) identify.

disclosure of their subject matter. Recall Heidegger's remarks from *HCT* 3 that in crises, scientists "reclaim" their subject matter "originally," and that such research "assumes a philosophical cast." The result, when successful, is a scientific revolution, the experience of which Kuhn, following Hanson, likens to a *Gestalt* switch:[109] not just this or that phenomenon but, rather, a whole domain of phenomena now appears in a radically new light.

No longer judging the success of their research by extant norms, the scientist must now adopt a thoroughly first-person stance toward themselves: they must take self-ownership in venturing a resolute decision about their subject matter. Following his remark about the anonymity and interchangeability of (normal) scientific work, quoted earlier, Heidegger claims that philosophical work – undertaken, as we have seen, by scientists in crisis – "is never a mere duplicate" and demands that "everyone is in themselves whole and unique" (GA27 226). Resolute decisions require us to acknowledge existential death, i.e., the ever-looming threat that our pursuits and our corresponding identities will dissolve. As Kuhn and Feyerabend point out – and as the case of Barbara McClintock illustrates – norm-challenging research initially raises far more problems than it solves, its ultimate success is far from guaranteed, and its proponents are frequently viewed by their colleagues with suspicion.[110] But by rendering a resolute decision, the scientist achieves authenticity and offers a revolutionary disclosure of their subject matter.

4.3 Science's Epistemic and Ethical Significance

In the aftermath of a scientific revolution, a new positivistic consolidation phase of research emerges. Hence, the cycle continues: as historical falling sets in, access to reality must eventually be re-established via a new ontological disclosure; authenticity in science must be "repeatedly retrieved." We thus can now more fully appreciate Heidegger's remark from GA27 quoted earlier:

> [S]cience should never be equated with its results, results that are then passed from hand to hand . . . . [W]hat is essential to science [lies] . . . rather in that which is appropriated ever anew. (32)

Mature scientific research, for Heidegger, does not, and ought not, deliver us ever more secure theories, as SCS would suggest; instead, since its aim is opening up access to reality (following ACS), it issues in cyclical crises that lead to renewed, potentially revolutionary ontological reflection. Scientists therefore must "appropriate" their subject matter "ever anew"; and in so

---

[109] Kuhn (2012, pp. 85, 112–14). Kuhn takes this analogy from Hanson (1958).

[110] See Section 3.2.2. See also Feyerabend's famous account of Galileo (1993, pp. 77–146) as well as Kuhn (2012, pp. 105, 156–57).

doing, they take ownership of their research and achieve authenticity. It is in this sense that science is Dasein's existential possibility of "being-in-the-truth" and "has its origin in authentic existence" (*SZ* 363); for Heidegger, science thus is an epistemically *and* ethically privileged pursuit.

5 Continuity and Development in the Later Heidegger's Approach to Science

The later Heidegger's discussions of science exhibit many key developments, not least of which is a markedly more pessimistic tone. However, whereas some scholars frame his later analysis of science as a departure from his earlier views,[111] I contend that his core commitments remain largely consistent. Indeed, I will argue that the later Heidegger's approach to science is best seen as sharpening and slightly modifying, rather than abandoning, his earlier critique of SCS and support for ACS; his shift in tone and focus betrays his growing worry that SCS has gained currency not only in philosophy, but in science itself. And when science is no longer primarily concerned with gaining (and regaining) access to reality, he worries that its proper distinction from other technical pursuits (such as engineering, business, and public policy) begins to dissolve.

There are three major developments in Heidegger's later writings on science: (1) his critique of modern science's quantitative orientation, (2) his analysis of the "industry" (*Betrieb*) of science, and (3) the emergence of his concept of technology as the final age in the history of Western metaphysics. Section 5.1 only briefly touches on (1), which deserves an independent treatment.[112] Section 5.2 discusses (2) at length. Finally, Section 5.3 briefly gestures toward (3), which Section 6 treats in detail.

First, however, let me indicate the continuity in Heidegger's basic commitments by dissecting the slogan he coins to analyze modern science in his 1953 SR, which is perhaps his most sustained later discussion of science.

5.1 "Science Is the theory of the actual"

"[T]hat in which the essence of science lies . . . may be expressed in one concise statement. It runs: *Science is the theory of the actual* [*Wirklichen*]" (SR 157). Heidegger immediately adds that "science" here refers to *modern* science rather than to its medieval or ancient predecessors.

---

[111] See Rouse (1985a, p. 207), Rouse (1985b, pp. 76, 79), and Rouse (2005, pp. 181–86). Rouse's contention is rooted in his commitment to the presence-at-hand–centric interpretation of the early Heidegger that I criticize in Section 2.4. See also Glazebrook (2000, pp. 5–10), Caputo (2012), and Wendland (2019).

[112] Some of the most relevant comments on (1) can be found in *QT* 58–64, *P* 235, *CP* 117, SR 170, *OBT* 65–66, *EN* 116.

Heidegger's essay then unfolds, characteristically, with an etymologically informed analysis of "theory" and "the actual." I must pass over a detailed treatment of the various turns in his analysis. Key for our purposes is that these terms respectively refer to what Heidegger calls "entrapping and securing representing" and "objecthood" (*Gegenständigkeit*), which indicate what he believes to be modern science's epistemological and ontological commitments.[113] Let me briefly unpack each notion, beginning with the latter.

Just after introducing the term "objecthood," Heidegger writes that "what presences becomes an object for a setting-before, a representing [*Vor-stellen*]" (SR 163). In other words, under a metaphysics of "objecthood," to be is to be an *object* that is available to a representing *subject*. Objects have several key features.

(1) *Objects occupy stable roles within an efficient causal sequence.* Heidegger stresses how reality (or "the actual," i.e., "what presences as self-exhibiting" (SR 167)) "appears now in the in the light of the causality of the *causa efficiens*" (SR 161; see also QCT 7, 26), or how for modern science, "the actual will exhibit itself as an interacting network, i.e., in surveyable series of related causes" (SR 168).

(2) *Objects behave according to precise, ideally mathematical laws.* Heidegger observes that "the possibilities for the posing of questions" about objects in a given field of science is "map[ped] out in advance," such that "[e]very new phenomenon emerging within an area of science is refined to such a point that it fits into the normative objective coherence of the theory" (SR 169; his remarks on mathematics on SR 170, quoted and discussed in a moment, are also relevant).

(3) *The existence of a given object is intersubjectively verifiable by following a set of privileged, specified procedures.* Under a metaphysics of object-hood, Heidegger claims that reality now appears to be what "stand[s] firm as guaranteed" (SR 162). "The actual, he writes, "thus becomes *surveyable* and *capable of being followed out* in its sequences. The actual becomes *secured* in its objecthood" (SR 168, emphasis added). Or as he writes in *OBT*, "procedure secures for itself, within the realm of being, its sphere of objects" (59).

Meanwhile, "entrapping and securing representing" is the epistemological counterpart to a metaphysics of objecthood (SR 168). It is characterized by

---

[113] We will see in Section 6 that Heidegger thinks quantum physics in fact jettisons these commitments in favor of a metaphysics of "resourcehood" (*Beständigkeit*) and an epistemology of "enframing" (*Ge-stell*). Nevertheless, as I will demonstrate, this development only exacerbates his underlying worry that the cyclical ontological disclosures proper to science qua ACS will come to fade from actual scientific practice.

the aim to *make* entities fit within a "surveyable series of related causes." We might thus say that under these epistemological commitments, subjects *know* objects when the latter are assigned roles within efficient causal sequences and behave according to laws that are intersubjectively verifiable via favored procedures – i.e., when they can be "entrapped" and "secured" within an ordered representational framework.[114]

> An oft-cited statement of Max Planck reads: "The actual is [*Wirklich ist*] what can be measured." This means that the decision about what may pass in science, in this case in physics, for assured knowledge rests with the measurability supplied in the objecthood of nature and ... in the possibilities inherent in the measuring procedure. The statement of Max Planck ... articulates something that belongs to the essence of modern science, not merely to physical science. The methodology, characterized by entrapping securing ... is a calculating [*Berechnen*]. We should not ... understand this term in the narrow sense of performing an operation with numbers. To calculate [*Rechnen*], in the broad, essential sense, means: to reckon [*rechnen*] with something, i.e., to take it into account; to count [*rechnen*] on something, i.e., to set it up as an object of expectation. (SR 169–70)

Heidegger thus claims that modern science generally is "mathematical" in a broad sense: it aims at

> the harmonizing of all relations of order ... and therefore "calculates" [*rechnet*] in advance with one fundamental equation for all merely possible ordering. (SR 170; see also SR 172)

Heidegger suggests here that the reason mathematical physics is considered exemplary among the sciences is because we have tacitly accepted a metaphysics of objecthood and an epistemology of entrapping securing representing. Physics' success in producing quantitative predictions and explanations (i.e., its *mathematics* in the familiar, narrow sense) is an especially potent example of "mathematics" in the broad sense: rendering reality surveyable as a sequence of anticipated effects. Moreover, he suggests that what we now commonly refer to as a "theory of everything" (ToE) – i.e., "a set of equations capable of describing all phenomena that have been observed, or that will ever be observed" (Laughlin and Pines 2000, p. 28) – remains the holy grail of physics because it epitomizes what he sees as the regulative epistemic ideal of modern science: the creation of a "knowledge map" or "world picture" so secure that, for any legitimate theoretical question, the correct answer could be produced algorithmically.[115]

---

[114] SR 161–62, 166–70; see also *OBT* 59–69.

[115] See *CP* 116 and *OBT* 64–71; Heidegger himself uses the map metaphor in a strikingly similar way on *IM* 12.

Heidegger claims not only that these metaphysical and epistemological commitments are historically novel – they "would have been as strange to medieval man as [they] would have been dismaying to Greek thought" (SR 168) – but also that they severely restrict our disclosive range in modernity. For example, consider that Augustine (despite his express opposition to skepticism) repeatedly stresses that what is most real – namely, God – escapes our efforts at clear and comprehensive representation.[116]

> He [God] now appears to us clouded in mystery . . . not as he really is[.]
> . . . You [God] alone know yourself completely as you are . . . . It does not seem right in your presence that the unchanging Light should be known, in the same way it knows itself, by the changeable being it casts light on. (*Confessions* 13.15.18–13.16.19)

The basic commitments of modern science render it impossible to countenance such an entity. More broadly, they render it impossible to countenance any entity that is recalcitrant to the currently favored representational frameworks.

Heidegger's remarks thus amount to an elaboration (indeed, a deepening) of his earlier commitments. Under the reigning ontological and epistemological commitments, Heidegger observes, the aim of science is understood to be developing a set of theories so secure as to transform inquiry into a matter of calculation rather than opening up and maintaining access to reality (principally via cyclical, revolutionary ontological disclosures, which upset extant theories). ACS, he worries, is increasingly losing ground to SCS. As we will presently see, Heidegger thinks this trend means that science proper might eventually cease to exist.

5.2 A Key Development: Heidegger on the "Industry" (*Betrieb*) of Science

5.2.1 What Is Betrieb?

Betrieb has two relevant senses for Heidegger: "business" and "bustle." A *Betrieb* is an economic enterprise; but *Betrieb* can also signify a flurry of activity. I translate it as "industry" to capture both senses: Heidegger's point is that science has become *an industry*, i.e., just another economic sector – devoted to the manufacture of useful information rather than, e.g., textiles, and carried out almost entirely within strictly defined institutions (universities, research institutes, academic publishers). Meanwhile, these institutions press scientists, like workers in other fields, to be *industrious*.[117] Scientists constantly define and

---

[116] For Augustine's opposition to skepticism, see *Against the Academicians*.

[117] Heidegger's chief analysis of the concept of *Betrieb* occurs in *OBT* 63–65, 73–74; see also *CP* 113–24, SR 169–71.

research new puzzles and regularly disseminate their findings at conferences and in journals – which stokes new puzzles and research, and so on, *ad infinitum*.

Heidegger's analysis of the industry of science helps him resolve a puzzle: he claims that science, guided by the ideal of a conclusive "world picture," aims at *stasis* – i.e., at securing a conclusive, comprehensive theory that renders inquiry a matter of calculation. Yet a glance at actual science reveals that research is constantly in motion, defining and resolving ever new puzzles. As Max Weber observes, scientists are doomed to see their work become obsolete within years of publication (and often much sooner).[118] How does Heidegger square this fact with his theory?

The concept of industry allows Heidegger to maintain that science's constant "motion," or progress, is a perverse consequence of its driving aim to arrive at a terminus of knowledge. Scientists press forward *within* a going ontological framework, with the aim of refining its theoretical articulation and improving its empirical coverage. Meanwhile, they generally avoid ontological reflection, since a new disclosure threatens to upset the going theories.

Once again, Heidegger anticipates Kuhn. Progress in research occurs above all when foundational issues are assiduously avoided. Once a set of basic concepts has sufficiently established itself, scientists can apply themselves to the specialized problems that characterize Kuhnian "normal science." Thus, specialization, born of tenacity to the going assumptions – which Heidegger characterizes as science's "having-to-be-based on its own results" (*OBT* 63) – is the chief cause of scientific progress; and such progress is incentivized by scientific institutions.[119]

But the later Heidegger's view is also importantly different from Kuhn's – and, strikingly, from his own earlier account in *SZ* discussed in Section 4. Like Kuhn, the early Heidegger thinks science consists in (1) a positivistic consolidation phase, which cyclically engenders its own dissolution in (2) a revolutionary crisis phase characterized by renewed ontological reflection. But later, he worries that science will remain permanently stuck in phase (1).

What motivates Heidegger's later, pessimistic view? He thinks the industry of science incentivizes an inattentiveness to ontology bordering on indifference, which makes disclosure a remote possibility:

> Industry becomes mere industry [*bloßen Betrieb*] when its methodology no longer holds itself open on the basis of an ever new completion of its projection, but rather leaves this behind as something simply given and no

---

[118] Weber (2004, p. 11).   [119] *OBT* 63–64, *CP* 114.

longer ever requiring confirmation; instead, all it does is to chase after results piling on top of each other and their calculation. (*OBT* 74)

I will now dive deeper into this contention. Insofar as science becomes "mere industry," it ceases being science proper at all. Consequently, its dual epistemic and ethical significance (i.e., the possibility it affords for a special kind of flourishing – namely, authenticity – achieved in ontological disclosures) begins to erode.

5.2.2 Epistemic and Ethical Implications

Heidegger argues that we pursue science from *wonder*, evoked in response to an experience of what he calls "the nothing," which occasions us to engage in the kind of ontological reflection that leads to a new disclosure of being – and subsequently, not only to a new research program, but also to a new set of social possibilities.

> Only if science exists on the basis of metaphysics can it fulfill in ever-renewed ways its essential task, which is not to amass and classify bits of knowledge, but to disclose in ever-renewed fashion the entire expanse of truth in nature and history.
>
> Only because the nothing is manifest in the ground of Dasein can the total strangeness of beings overwhelm us. Only when the strangeness of beings oppresses us does it arouse and evoke wonder. Only on the ground of wonder – the manifestness of the nothing – does the "why?" loom before us. Only because the "why" is possible as such can we in a definite way inquire into the grounds and ground things. Only because we can question and ground things is the destiny of our existence placed in the hands of the researcher. (*P* 95–96)

"The nothing" refers to an experience of cosmic emptiness that discloses being itself. When we consider the question *Why is there something rather than nothing?*, we come to appreciate (1) *that* there is anything at all and (2) the contingency of everything (after all, why are things like *this* and not in some other way?). "The strangeness of beings" – what he earlier called *uncanniness*, the stubborn mysteriousness or openness of reality – gives rise to the felt demand to investigate, and hence, to science.

Science proper remains open to its founding ontological disclosure by seeing the possibilities for uncovering that it affords.[120] But a research program remains meaningful only to the extent that the experience of wonder remains alive; as Heidegger writes, "scientific existence is possible only if in advance it holds itself out into the nothing" (*P* 95).[121] His implication, let me suggest, is

---

[120] See Heidegger's comments on academic history in *IM* 48.   [121] See also *HCCR* 31, *IM* 7.

that the wonder that sustains science depends on a *disposition of ontological openness* – the recognition that what lies disclosed and uncovered before us is contingent, that it's possible that things could be different from how they appear to be, or that there could be nothing at all.[122]

It's worth noting that Heidegger's analysis strikingly parallels Paul Feyerabend's claim that *counterinduction* serves an important role for science. Counterinduction is a *"pluralistic methodology"* that "introduce[s] and elaborate[s] hypotheses which are inconsistent with well-established theories and/or well-established facts" (1993, pp. 20–21). Feyerabend claims counterinduction is justified both critically and hermeneutically: it helps us identify our current theories' limitations and, just as importantly, their presuppositions – for "how can we possibly . . . analyze the terms in which we habitually express our most simple and straightforward observations, and reveal their presuppositions?" (1993, p. 22).

If we are not open to alternative disclosures, then we will cease attending to our current ontological assumptions. This inattentiveness, for Heidegger, is precisely what the industry of science demands. In this situation, puzzle-solving research becomes dislodged from its original, guiding aim of opening up access to reality. Instead, it becomes pursued, perplexingly, for its own sake, or else for the sake of its instrumental value in enhancing our control over a given domain. "From an inner compulsion," Heidegger writes,

> the researcher presses forward into the sphere occupied by the figure of, in the essential sense, the technologist. Only in this way can he remain capable of being effective, and only then, in the eyes of his age, is he real. (*OBT* 64)

Modern scientists, discouraged from maintaining an ontologically open disposition, are prevented from experiencing the wonder that occasions true science. Heidegger's worry is that science proper will "be dissolved" as it attains "industrial inconspicuousness" (*CP* 122). In other words, "science" will lose its distinction from other technical occupations, and the "scientist" will become merely a species of the technologist or technician (*Techniker*); science then will "have to withdraw into the public anonymity of all socially useful work" (*OBT* 65).

Increasingly, Heidegger worries, scientists will seek to augment our control over reality rather than to open up access to it. With this shift, the possibility for flourishing that science affords will be foreclosed.

---

[122] See *IM* 31–34 on the "oscillation" of entities between being and non-being. The specific sense of possibility at issue demands a detailed treatment that I cannot provide here.

5.3 Ontological Indifference in the Age of Technology

Ontological inquiry is the "essential task" of science proper; it thus has priority over specialized research puzzles. Ontological disclosures open up access to reality in the most fundamental way; research puzzles emerge as the scientist investigates the possibilities for uncovering that a given disclosure affords. Thus, ontological inquiry grounds and guides specialized research. But as research on specialized puzzles becomes dislodged from its proper aim of opening up access to reality, ontology undergoes, to borrow from Quine, "a humiliating demotion" (1983, p. 501). We thus become not only *inattentive* but also *indifferent* to ontology. Ontological inquiry – attending to our ontological assumptions – for the sake of ensuring that they are cogent, coherent, and hence, genuinely disclosive, is seen as worthless; ontological inquiry is, at best, valuable only instrumentally, insofar as our "framework" can help or hinder our puzzle-solving capabilities, and thus can enhance our control over a given domain.

Heidegger suspects that this indifference betrays a suppressed ontological assumption. By the middle of the twentieth century, he believes, modern science has come under the aegis of "the age of technology," the final stage in the history of Western metaphysics. In this age, being is no longer conceived in terms of the sort of mind-independence and amenability to mathematical modeling that Heidegger earlier dubbed "presence-at-hand"; rather, to be is now to be exploitable as a *resource* (*Bestand*) for the sake of unceasing human power-enhancement.

Indeed, as I will presently discuss in Section 6, Heidegger comes to believe that the emergence of quantum physics in the early and middle twentieth century depended on the age of technology's characteristic ontological indifference and commitment to an ontology of "resourcehood" (*Beständigkeit*).

6 Heidegger and Heisenberg on Quantum Physics, Science, Technology, and Modernity

Werner Heisenberg figures as the implicit interlocutor in QCT and SR, two of the later Heidegger's most important essays. Both were delivered as part of a 1953 public dialogue with Heisenberg on quantum physics and modernity (Heidegger circulated and read SR in advance to a small group, and he delivered QCT at the event itself).[123] This event was the culmination of a decades-long dialogue. Heidegger met Heisenberg at his hut in Todtnauberg for a multi-day discussion in 1935, and the two continued to engage each other over the next

---

[123] Carson (2010a, p. 493). Note that Heidegger's (1953) address is a revised version of an earlier address delivered in 1949 (published in *BFL* 23–43).

two decades. In fact, Heidegger was apparently the only non-scientist to whom Heisenberg regularly sent copies of his essays.[124]

Heidegger was the instigating force behind the 1953 event, and SR and QCT are manifestly in dialogue with Heisenberg and his contribution.[125] Heidegger even reportedly told a colleague, "[w]hat matters to me above all else is that *Heisenberg* hear" his remarks (Carson 2010b, p. 110). The emergence of quantum physics and Heisenberg's reflections on its significance profoundly influenced Heidegger's thinking.[126]

But what kind of influence did Heisenberg exert? Most scholars claim that the influence was primarily negative: on their reading, Heidegger opposes Heisenberg's views that quantum physics depends on metaphysical and epistemological commitments that are fundamentally distinct from those of classical physics, and that these new commitments inform a distinct late modern age. I disagree. I argue that Heidegger is positively disposed toward Heisenberg's claims, and in fact appropriates them to articulate his own account of modern technology as a distinct late modern age. Their disagreement, I argue, is limited; it concerns the depth and durability of the negative implications of quantum physics and late modernity for human flourishing.

Section 6.1 reviews Heisenberg's key claims from his 1953 address. Section 6.2 canvasses the extant scholarship on Heidegger's response, which reads him as largely disagreeing with Heisenberg's claims. Section 6.3 unpacks Heidegger's positive reception and appropriation of Heisenberg's claims. For Heidegger, the classical-quantum shift in physics betokens a shift in epoch-making metaphysical and epistemological commitments – from, as he puts it, *objecthood* (*Gegenständigkeit*) to *resourcehood* (*Beständigkeit*). But this shift, as we will see, only exacerbates Heidegger's concern that science is becoming increasingly indifferent to ontological inquiry in favor of developing increasingly powerful models; here too, then, Heidegger critiques the influence of SCS over scientific practice. Section 6.4 examines where Heidegger and Heisenberg disagree. Heidegger, I will argue, has a bleaker take on the ethical implications of quantum physics, late modern science, and the age of technology.

---

[124] See Carson (2010a, p. 491) and Carson (2010b, p. 90).

[125] Published as Heisenberg (1958a).

[126] This suffices to refute a falsehood promulgated by Richardson (1968, pp. 535–36) and echoed by Heelan (1995, p. 581). They claim that Heidegger's philosophy of science is obsolete because it's largely directed at classical physics and ignores modern physics.

6.1 Heisenberg's Claims

Heisenberg makes a bold claim toward the beginning of his remarks:

> [T]he changes in the foundations of modern science are an indication of profound transformations in the fundamentals of our existence, which on their part certainly have their effects in all areas of human experience. (Heisenberg 1958a, p. 95)

Quantum theory undermines the metaphysical assumptions that undergird classical physics. And the new metaphysics demanded by quantum physics is both a cause and a consequence of a broader historical shift whereby humans increasingly come to see their products, activities, and interests reflected in the world.

Heisenberg thinks classical physics is premised on the subject-object dichotomy and the corollary concept of "objectivity." As Scholasticism waned, nature was increasingly regarded as independent of both divine will and human concerns. The aim of classical physics was thus to study nature "in itself": we aim to be *objective* in our studies and to limit the influence of our *subjective* biases as much as possible (1958a, p. 96). "To the nineteenth century," Heisenberg elaborates,

> nature appeared as a lawful process in space and time, in whose description it was possible to ignore as far as axioms were concerned, even if not in practice, both man and his interference in nature. (Heisenberg 1958a, p. 98)

A foundational assumption of classical physics is that nature exists mind-independently; to study it properly, therefore, we ought to guard vigilantly against the influence of our subjective biases.

Classical physics also conceives of objective reality as atomistic. Atoms – or, later, subatomic particles – are considered to be "the intrinsically real" or "the final objective reality" (1958a, p. 99). Everything in nature reduces to these "smallest building blocks of matter": "through their mutual arrangement and motion, [atoms] call forth the colorful phenomena of our sense world" (1958a, pp. 98–99). Therefore, when we have a proper understanding of the behavior of elementary particles, we will thereby have attained objective knowledge about the most fundamental aspect of nature.

It thus came as a shock when researchers discovered that elementary particles appeared not to behave mind-independently. Heisenberg remarks:

> [F]or the smallest building blocks of matter every process of observation causes a major disturbance . . . . In consequence, we are finally led to believe that the laws of nature which we formulate mathematically in quantum theory deal no longer with the particles themselves but with our knowledge of the

elementary particles .... The conception of the objective reality of the elementary particles has thus evaporated in a curious way ... into the transparent clarity of a mathematics that represents no longer the behavior of the elementary particles but rather our knowledge of this behavior. (Heisenberg 1958a, pp. 99–100)

On Heisenberg's interpretation, a basic implication of quantum mechanics is that there is no clear boundary between observer and observed. As a result,

The familiar classification of the world into subject and object ... somehow no longer quite applies .... In science, also, the object of research is no longer nature itself but rather nature exposed to man's questioning, and to this extent man here also meets himself. (Heisenberg 1958a, pp. 104–05)

This final sentence is especially significant; Heisenberg claims that the broader historical shift he spoke of earlier as "profound transformations in the fundamentals of our existence" is best characterized by the claim that "for the first time in the course of history man on earth faces only himself ... he no longer finds any other partner or foe" (Heisenberg 1958a, p. 104).

Scientific technologies have transformed our relationship to nature. The science behind these technologies is so recondite that we feel "uncanny" or alienated from "natural experience" in our daily, technologically mediated interactions. Meanwhile, such technologies are so widespread that nearly every time we interact with nature we do so mediated through technology; therefore, increasingly, our encounters with nature are simultaneously encounters with ourselves (1958a, pp. 101–2, 104).

Similarly, quantum physics transforms our relationship to nature: the old picture, on which nature was "a realm existing according to its own laws, and into which man somehow had to fit himself," is now obsolete (1958a, p. 104). Nature at the most fundamental level is apparently not independent of us in the way classical physics assumed. Heisenberg thus concludes: "The world view of natural science thus ceases to be a view of 'natural' science in its proper sense" (1958a, p. 107). Quantum physics is a science of us humans as much as of nature; there no longer is any room for nature "in itself" in science.

We might finally ask what Heisenberg thinks motivates this seismic shift in the aims and assumptions of physics. He hints at his answer in the long quotation earlier: "the transparent clarity of [the] mathematics." He later elaborates:

In quantum theory, we accepted the described situation when it became possible to represent it mathematically and when, therefore, in every case we could say clearly and without danger of logical contradiction how the result of an experiment would turn out. (1958a, p. 105)

Quantum theory surrenders "the earlier ideal" of an objective science (1958a, p. 105) because doing so increases the power of our mathematics: we can model and predict a more comprehensive set of physical phenomena with heretofore unseen quantitative precision. Heisenberg illustrates this tradeoff in a discussion elsewhere of Bohr's concept of complementarity: depending on the experiment, matter (or light) will behave as a particle or as a wave. "The[se] two pictures," Heisenberg writes, "are of course mutually exclusive"; but the "dualism ... is no longer a difficulty since we know from the mathematical formulation of the theory that contradictions cannot arise." Nevertheless, "[a] real difficulty ... arises ... when one asks the famous question: But what happens 'really' in an atomic event?" (Heisenberg 1958b, pp. 50–51).[127]

With this increase in our predictive and technological power over nature, Heisenberg claims, quantum physics betokens a new age that has provoked considerable anxiety. We experience a disturbing claustrophobia and pessimism in always confronting "ourselves." Like other thinkers on modernity, Heisenberg develops a metaphor likening inquiry to a voyage aboard a ship.[128] Previously, we were confident that we could navigate to unseen destinations and experience genuine discovery. Now, however, it's as if our ship

> has been so securely built of iron and steel that the needle of [our] compass no longer points to the north, but only toward the ship's mass of iron. With such a ship, no destination can be reached[.] (Heisenberg 1958a, p. 108)

The implication is that we have lost confidence that we can discover real features of nature, and thus the confidence that our knowledge is genuine – and hence, that it's capable of genuinely progressing. Nevertheless, Heisenberg hopes that "[t]o the extent that we reach clarity about this limit, the limit itself may furnish the first firm hold by which we can orient ourselves anew"; hence, perhaps "in the course of long stretches of time" we will find a new "common center" for our thoughts, which will alleviate our anxiety (1958a, p. 108).

Let me thus distill four claims from Heisenberg:

C1. The shift from classical to quantum physics betokens a new intellectual age shaped by unique metaphysical and epistemological assumptions.

C2. Quantum physics betokens this new intellectual age insofar as it forecloses the old ideal of "objectivity," or, rather, *scientific realism* as applied to nature, which held sway under classical physics. ("Scientific realism" here means the claim that the aim of science is the accurate representation of

---

[127] These quotations notwithstanding, Bokulich (2008, p. 96) points out that Heisenberg has considerable misgivings about Bohr's concept of complementarity.

[128] See, e.g., Bacon (2003, pp. 10–11), Nietzsche (1974, pp. 180–81, 371), and Quine (2013, pp. 3–4).

mind-independent reality – i.e., of what is the case independently of our conceiving it so – and, concomitantly, that successful scientific theories faithfully represent mind-independent reality.[129])

C3.   Quantum physics is willing to sacrifice scientific realism because doing so allows scientists to develop more powerful mathematical models – i.e., equations that allow us to generate more numerous, precise, and accurate predictions.

C4.   The new intellectual age betokened by the emergence of quantum physics has provoked considerable anxiety, but the depth and durability of this anxiety is unclear.

6.2 Heidegger's Response: The Dominant Reading

Heidegger, as I read him, is positively disposed toward Heisenberg's claims – especially C1-C3, which he takes on board in articulating his concept of modern technology. His disagreement concerns C4; Heidegger is less ambivalent and more pessimistic than Heisenberg. Most striking on my reading, thus, is the generative affinity between Heidegger's and Heisenberg's views.

But most commentators suggest that Heidegger disagrees with C1, Heisenberg's most fundamental claim; they read Heidegger as holding a largely deflationary view of quantum physics' metaphysical and epistemological significance. Some frame Heidegger as a deflationist without clearly acknowledging the countervailing evidence.[130] Others, meanwhile, acknowledge such evidence but argue that Heidegger's considered position is deflationary.[131]

An explanation of my disagreement with extant scholarship is in order. The basic problem is that Heidegger's writings on quantum physics are *prima facie* ambivalent. Some passages suggest deflationary disagreement with C1. For instance:

> To be sure, atomic physics is experimentally and calculably of a different sort than classical physics. Thought in terms of its essence, however, it nevertheless remains the same physics. (*BFL* 41)

Heidegger suggests here that despite their empirical and methodological differences, classical and quantum physics share the same basic philosophical commitments. Elsewhere, however, he states just the opposite:

---

[129] Van Fraassen (1980, pp. 6–9) offers the classic formulation of this concept of scientific realism.
[130] See, e.g., Kockelmans (1985, p. 169), Glazebrook (2000, pp. 249–51), and Watson (2012, pp. 47, 52–53, 55–56).
[131] See Seigfried (1990, pp. 626, 629), Chevalley (1992, pp. 342, 349, 352, 357–60), Ma and van Brakel (2014), and Carman (2019).

[T]he present leaders in atomic physics, Niels Bohr, and Heisenberg, think philosophically through and through, and only because of this do they create new ways of posing questions and above all hold out in questionability. (*QT* 45)

One response to this *prima facie* tension is to argue that Heidegger's views evolved, such that his position became more deflationary as he matured.[132] But Heidegger's most counter-deflationary remarks are found in some of his latest works (namely, his 1953 SR and QCT, his 1955–56 *PR*, and his 1969 *LT*); making matters worse, SR contains both deflationary *and* counter-deflationary remarks.

Carman (2019) and Ma and van Brakel (2014) take a more promising approach. They develop sophisticated interpretations under which Heidegger has a more or less consistent deflationary position. They allege that Heidegger allows for *lower-order* discontinuity between classical and quantum physics (and early and late modernity more broadly), which is nevertheless subsumed under a *higher-order* continuity, which renders their differences "secondary" to their commonalities (Carman 2019, p. 308). Carman thus claims:

> Notwithstanding ... occasional turns of phrase ... Heidegger consistently maintained that the dominant understanding of being remained essentially the same from the early 17th century to the present[.] (Carman 2019, p. 306)

I agree that Heidegger thinks that the epochal break betokened by the classical-quantum shift is of a lower order, and that, at a higher order, he sees continuity. But there's a crucial difference. Carman and Ma and van Brakel suggest that this higher-order continuity is, for Heidegger, a unique feature of modernity and explains an ambivalence he displays uniquely about early and late modernity. But I think Heidegger displays the same ambivalence for each pair of successive epochs in his "history of being"; each new epoch introduces deep qualitative shifts in metaphysical and epistemological commitments, but each shift develops by extrapolating latent tendencies in the prior epoch.[133] Furthermore, all epochs exist within a Western tradition that itself is unified by higher-order features.[134] Thus, the higher-order continuity Heidegger posits is a general feature of the history of Western metaphysics rather than a specific feature of modernity. Notwithstanding such continuity, then, I maintain, contrary to Carman and Ma and van Brakel, that early and late modernity constitute distinct

---

[132] See, e.g., Chevalley (1992).

[133] On the ancient-medieval shift, compare *P* 209 and QCT 6–12 with *SZ* 22–25; *BPP* 117–19; *OBT* 61, 68–69, 71; *QT* 45, 55, 61 and *EN* 180; on the medieval-early modern shift, compare *OBT* 61–62 and SR 168 with *SZ* 24–25; *IPR* 79, 116–23; *OBT* 81; and SR 161–62. See also *OBT* 11.

[134] See, e.g., SZ 21–27, *IPR* 83, *TB* 8–10, *IM* 64–65, 222–30, *EN* 164.

epochs in Heidegger's history of being on par with the ancient Greek and medieval epochs.

Nevertheless, properly litigating this debate would require a deep dive into Heidegger's philosophy of history and the relationship between technology and early modern metaphysics, matters which remain the subject of considerable scholarly dispute and require a detailed treatment in their own right that is beyond this project's scope.[135]

Next, I provide a sustained account of the substantial affinity between Heidegger's and Heisenberg's views, which the literature currently lacks.[136]

6.3 Heidegger on C1–C3

In *PR*, Heidegger affirms C1:

> The relation of the knowing subject [*erkennenden Subjekts*] to the object [*Objekt*] essentially changes ... in modern atomic physics. Parenthetically it should be mentioned that in modern atomic physics a transformation in the relation to objects [*Gegenständen*] is prepared [*vorbereitet*] that, on the way through modern technology, completely changes the manner of human representation [*Vorstellungsweise*]. (*PR* 7)

Quantum physics betokens the emerging age of "modern technology"; its key shift in metaphysics is its "transformation" of the subject-object relationship, which, in turn, has implications for epistemology. Here Heidegger gestures toward claims that he develops several years earlier for his public conversation with Heisenberg.

We will examine those in a moment. First, however, we must turn to a passage where Heidegger in fact makes one of his clearest and oft-cited expressions of *deflationary disagreement* with C1 and C2.[137]

> [M]odern nuclear and field physics *also* still remains physics – i.e., science, i.e., theory, which entraps objects belonging to the actual, in their objecthood, in order to secure them in the unity of objecthood.
>
> ... This rough indication of a distinction between epochs within modern physics makes plain where the change from the one to the other takes place: in

---

[135] For instance, Ma and van Brakel (2014, pp. 29–35) and Carman (2019, p. 306) argue for a single unified epoch of modernity, while Wrathall (2011, Chapter 10, esp. pp. 221, 226, 241) and Thomson (2011, pp. 8–9, 57–58) argue for distinct early modern and technological epochs of modernity.

[136] Carson (2010a, p. 494), Ihde (2010, pp. 107, 109–10), and perhaps also Pöggeler (1993, esp. pp. 24–29, 32–33) suggest non-deflationary readings of Heidegger's engagement with Heisenberg. But their chief interests lie elsewhere, and so they don't develop their interpretations at length.

[137] Deflationary readers who cite this passage include Kockelmans (1985, p. 169), Chevalley (1992, p. 343), Glazebrook (2000, p. 251), and Carman (2019, pp. 308–9).

the experience and determination of the objecthood wherein nature sets itself forth. Nevertheless, what does *not* change with this change from geometrizing-classical physics to nuclear and field physics is this: the fact that nature has in advance to set itself in place for the entrapping securing that science, as theory, accomplishes. (SR 172–73)

Recall the concepts of "objecthood" (*Gegenständigkeit*) and "entrapping and securing representing" introduced earlier.[138] Scientific realism remains a live possibility under these assumptions: theories and concepts are human constructions; nevertheless, it remains plausible to claim that the aim of such theories and concepts is to mirror a mind-independent realm of nature, such that successful theories faithfully represent that realm. In claiming that classical and quantum physics alike are characterized by a metaphysics of objecthood and an epistemology of entrapping and securing representing, Heidegger thus here denies C1 and C2. Remarkably, however, he dramatically reverses himself in his next breath:

> However, the way in which in the most recent phase of atomic physics even the *object vanishes also*, and the way in which, above all, the subject-object relation as pure relation thus takes precedence *over* the object and the subject, to become secured as resource, cannot be more precisely discussed in this place.

(Objecthood changes into the resourcehood of the resource [*Beständigkeit des Bestandes*], a resourcehood determined from out of enframing. {See "The Question Concerning Technology."} The subject-object relation thus reaches, for the first time, its pure "relational," i.e., ordering, character in which both the subject and the object are sucked up as resources. That does not mean that the subject-object relation vanishes, but rather the opposite: it now attains to its most extreme dominance, which is predetermined from out of enframing. It becomes a resource to be commanded and set in order.) (SR 173)[139]

The key remark here is Heidegger's claim that the classical-quantum shift betokens a shift from *objecthood* (*Gegenständigkeit*) to *resourcehood* (*Beständigkeit*). Both terms, and their related root words *object* (*Gegenstand*) and *resource* (*Bestand*), carry epochal significance for Heidegger.[140] For instance, in QCT, he writes:

---

[138] See Section 5.1.   [139] The reference in braces to QCT is Heidegger's own.

[140] Following Lovitt, Heidegger translators typically render *Bestand* as "standing-reserve." I think "resource" captures Heidegger's sense more intuitively. Meanwhile, *Beständigkeit* is introduced as a clear parallel for *Gegenständigkeit* (objecthood), which serves as an abstract generalization of *Gegenstand* (object). Hence "resourcehood" makes better sense here than a translation that would otherwise be more appropriate, such as "constancy" or "subsistence." The common root -*stand*, which Heidegger often emphasizes, is unfortunately lost in translation.

The name "resource" assumes the rank of an inclusive rubric. It designates nothing less than the way in which everything presences that is wrought upon by the challenging revealing. That which stands as resource [*Was im Sinne des Bestandes steht*] no longer stands over against us as object [*Gegenstand*]. (QCT 17)[141]

Heidegger thus endorses C1. And he hints as to how he will interpret C2 and C3: quantum physics betokens the late modern age of technology insofar as it relates to entities as *resources* rather than *objects*, and this shift has something to do with "ordering," "challenging," and "enframing." Several pages later, Heidegger elaborates in a reference to Heisenberg's remarks about the "uncanniness" of nature under modern science.[142]

If modern physics must resign itself ever increasingly to the fact that its realm of representation remains inscrutable and incapable of being visualized, this resignation is . . . challenged forth by the rule of enframing, which demands that nature be orderable as resource. (QCT 23)

Enframing (*Ge-stell*) is Heidegger's coinage for late modernity's unique epistemological commitment; we will return to it in a moment. For now, let me address the metaphysical commitment. The key questions are: (1) what distinguishes resourcehood from objecthood? And (2) how does the classical-quantum shift reflect the shift from objecthood to resourcehood? A passage from *LT* addresses (1) and is worth quoting at length:

The manner of this sending [i.e., the metaphysics of the post-Scholastic epoch] is *objecthood* [*Gegenständlichkeit*] (as the objective being of the object). Now the further that modern technology unfolds, the more does objecthood transform into *resourcehood* [*Beständlichkeit*] (into a holding-at-one's-disposal). Already today there are no longer objects (no beings, insofar as these would stand against a subject taking them into view) – there are now only resources (beings that are held in readiness for being consumed) . . .. Everything (beings as a whole) from the outset arranges itself in the horizon of utility . . . the *orderability* of what is to be seized. The forest ceases to be an object (as it was for the scientists of the eighteenth and nineteenth centuries), and becomes, for the human – finally stepping forth in his true form as technologist, i.e., for the human who a priori sees the particular being in the horizon of usability – a "greenspace." It can no longer appear in the objective [*gegenständlichen*] neutrality of an over against [*Gegenüber*]. There is no longer anything other than resources: stock, supplies, means.

---

[141] For similar remarks, see SR 173; QCT 19, 23, 26–27; *BFL* 41; *Z* 213; and *LT* 61–62.
[142] "Uncanniness" here should not be confused with Heidegger's concept of existential uncanniness discussed earlier.

> The ontological determination of resource (of the being as material supply) is ... orderability, the constant possibility of being summoned and ordered, that is, the persistent standing-at-one's-disposal. (*LT* 61–62)[143]

Recall that objecthood leaves room for scientific realism. The objects we investigate maintain an "objective neutrality" vis-à-vis us: they plausibly furnish reality independently of our schemes and aims (e.g., forests). But resources are *dependent* on our schemes and aims (e.g., greenspaces, which exist only due to urban planning): they are a "means," "orderable," "held in readiness for being consumed," or (as he says elsewhere) "completely unautonomous" (QCT 17). More precisely, resources are essentially *instrumental* and *schematized*: their existence depends on an artificial scheme of production or consumption within which they serve a role and on the basis of which they can be deployed. Hence, they do not furnish mind-independent reality. Scientific realism would thus be a nonstarter under a metaphysics of resourcehood. Meanwhile, the epistemological commitment of *enframing* is now legible: in the age of technology, we *know* something as a resource when we are able to fit it within a production or consumption scheme such as to exploit its instrumental value.

This will have to suffice for an answer to question (1). The answer to (2), meanwhile, lies in C2 and C3. Quantum physics, as Heisenberg understands it, requires us to forego scientific realism for the sake of increased predictive power. Heidegger thinks this tradeoff carries epochal significance. Once we have made it, he suggests, we have eliminated the conceptual gap between science and engineering. That is to say, physics no longer primarily aims to know nature for its own sake; instead, it now aims, above all, to manipulate nature – paradigmatically in the form of experimentation.[144]

Heidegger elaborates in *Z* and *LT*. For classical physics, "space and its characteristics are viewed as actually existing" – "[o]ne can still have an intuition of Newtonian space." By contrast, quantum physics employs "models" that are understood to "ha[ve] a merely instrumental character" – they are held to be valuable just insofar as they yield accurate quantitative predictions, insofar as they allow us to "identically repea[t] an experiment within the schema of 'if x ... then y'."[145]

---

[143] See also Heidegger's example of the aircraft on QCT 17.

[144] The infamous slogan "Shut up and calculate!" provides corroborating evidence for Heidegger's view. This slogan has often been invoked to describe the ethos of much physics research in the latter half of the twentieth century, according to which physicists were discouraged from inquiring into the conceptual foundations of quantum mechanics and encouraged, instead, simply to use it. See Carroll (2019a) and Carroll (2019b, pp. 1–10, 27–31) for helpful background and commentary.

[145] *Z* 213–14, *LT* 53–54.

According to one model, one can calculate location; according to another model, velocity. Where objects have become inaccessible to intuition, and where, nevertheless, the necessity for calculability is maintained, the model comes into play. When the experimental machinery necessarily changes the objects, then one still has only the change in hand and no longer the object. Has the object become inaccessible to intuition? Only in physics is the concept of a model meaningful. *Where a model appears, the projection [of nature] still has a merely instrumental character, but no longer an ontological character.* (Z 213–14, italics mine)

Similarly, on *LT* 54, Heidegger reportedly claims that "the concept of theory developed by Newton and Galileo stands in the middle between *theoria* in the Greek sense and the contemporary significance of the word." The passage continues:

From the Greek interpretation, this concept retains an ontological view of nature, which is regarded as the totality of movement in space and time. Opposed to this, the contemporary theory gives up this ontological tendency; it is solely the establishing of the elements required for an experiment, or, if one prefers, the operating instructions for carrying out an experiment. (*LT* 54)

The decisive shift between classical and quantum physics, Heidegger suggests, lies in the latter's ontological indifference and, concomitantly, its renouncing of scientific realism. Recall Heisenberg's admission that quantum physics' ontological presuppositions are incoherent, and hence, not robustly disclosive.[146] If one accepts scientific realism, then this situation would be alarming and demand resolution; after all, one cannot possibly represent mind-independent reality faithfully if one's ontological assumptions are incoherent. Scientific realism, which remained plausible under classical physics, thus demands that scientists *not* be indifferent to ontology. But research in quantum physics pressed forward all the same. It thus made an epochal break in being manifestly premised on ontological indifference; it forswears scientific realism – and does so, moreover, for the sake of enhanced predictive power.

Therefore, for quantum physics, "nature" is conceptualized under resource-hood rather than objecthood: natural phenomena can no longer be understood to reflect a mind-independent realm governed by laws that our equations purport to represent. Rather, natural phenomena serve as instruments for producing successful experiments, and our mathematical models purport merely to facilitate such success. Heidegger thus endorses and appropriates C1-C3 in developing his claim that we are in a new epoch characterized by resourcehood rather than objecthood.

---

[146] See especially Heisenberg (1958b, pp. 50–51), quoted in Section 6.1.

But the joint revolutionary developments in late modern science (quantum physics) and metaphysics (the age of technology) ultimately entrench, in a newly potent form, SCS over ACS. Classical physics, on account of retaining an "ontological" view of nature that allows for scientific realism, was still partially informed by ACS; quantum physics, which discards this in favor of an "instrumental" view of nature, more decisively entrenches SCS. In 1929, Heidegger claims that ontological disclosure is the "essential task" of science (*P* 95); but in the ensuing years, he comes to worry that ontological indifference has begun to take hold, such that the aim of science is now more than ever understood to be developing increasingly comprehensive, predictive models rather than opening up access to reality.

6.4 Heidegger on Quantum Theory's Perverse Ethical Implications in the Age of Technology

As we discussed earlier, Heisenberg acknowledges that quantum theory and the age it betokens have provoked considerable anxiety, but he hopes that this anxiety will prove short lived. Heidegger is more gravely concerned. He thinks that quantum theory, as Heisenberg articulates it, furthers the process that eventuates in us taking ourselves to be resources:

> Through Heisenberg's indeterminacy relation the human finally is explicitly integrated in the artificiality of the instruments and has become a piece of this resource. Seen as such, he can encounter only himself in all objects – but what is the "he himself" there? (Instrumentation!) (GA7 57)[147]

Heisenberg claims that quantum theory shows that we "encounter ourselves" in our interactions with the smallest building blocks of nature. Heidegger's reply is that we encounter "ourselves" in such experiments only through the influence of our measuring instruments. Heidegger thus perceives in Heisenberg's view an unwitting equation of humanity with such instruments, which betrays that we now understand ourselves to be resources. QCT elaborates on this claim:

> [W]hen destining reigns in the mode of enframing, it is the supreme danger ... As soon as what is unconcealed no longer concerns man even as object, but does so, rather, exclusively as resource, and man in the midst of objectlessness is nothing but the orderer of the resource, then ... he comes to the point where he himself will have to be taken as resource. Meanwhile man, precisely as the one so threatened, exalts himself to the posture of lord of the earth. In this way the impression [*Anschein*] comes to prevail that everything

---

[147] See also Heidegger's 1954 note to a similar effect in GA90 297 (cited in Carman 2019, p. 310). In these passages, Heidegger apparently reverses his position as expressed in a set of notes from 1937 (GA76 179–81).

man encounters exists only insofar as it is his construct. This impression [*Anschein*] gives rise in turn to one final deceptive appearance [*trügerischen Schein*]: It seems as though man everywhere and always encounters only himself. Heisenberg has with complete correctness pointed out that the actual must present itself to contemporary man in this way. *In truth, however, precisely nowhere does man today any longer encounter himself, i.e., his essence.* Man . . . fails to see himself as the one spoken to, and hence also fails in every way to hear in what respect he ek-sists, from out of his essence, in the realm of an exhortation or address, and thus *can never* encounter only himself. (QCT 26–27)

I pointed out earlier that quantum theory, as Heidegger hears Heisenberg articulate it, arises from and reinforces the "technological" assumptions of resourcehood and enframing, under which we understand everything – including ourselves – to be resources awaiting deployment for the sake of continual human power enhancement. The irony, for Heidegger, is that quantum physics' apparently human-empowering features come about as a result of losing a sense of the unique ontological character of humanity qua Dasein. Let me elaborate.

Heidegger's concept of "ek-sistence" (literally, "standing-outside") refers, above all, to his commitment to Dasein's *ontological receptivity*: we essentially do not *bestow* but rather *reveal* or *disclose* ontological significance (*that* and *how* beings are).[148] We are "in the realm of an exhortation or address," receptive to rather than generative of being.[149] Hence man "*can never* encounter only himself."

But Heisenbergian quantum theory's rejection of scientific realism promotes the view that "everything man encounters exists only insofar as it is his construct" such that "man everywhere and always encounters only himself" – in which case, reality as we encounter it reflects us, i.e., our *assignments* of ontological significance. In other words, it promotes the "impression" or "deceptive appearance" that we are not ontologically receptive – i.e., that we in fact *do* bestow ontological significance.

Heisenbergian quantum theory, for Heidegger, thus betokens a historical age in which humanity has lost a sense of itself as Dasein – and indeed, has come to see both itself and everything else as merely different kinds of resources. Let me unpack this final point.

A core perversity of modern technology's characteristic instrumental logic, for Heidegger, is that it has become dislodged from any intrinsic end that would promote human flourishing – after all, modern technological assumptions leave us bereft of the sort of robust concept of human existence needed to anchor an

---

[148] This complex notion is best developed in "Letter on 'Humanism'" (see *P* 246–76).
[149] See, e.g., SR 182 and *P* 246–52.

account of human flourishing. Technological instrumentalization, then, merely serves the end of further instrumentalization, i.e., a continual expansion of humanity's range of manipulative control, to be exercised for no other end than to promote further control (*BFL* 28). But in that case, since any given means is defined by its end, a palpable emptiness and absurdity suffuses our relationships with all things (which are, so to speak, "pure means").[150] Indeed, Heidegger stresses that every being comes to seem fungible and disposable (*LT* 62): everything, including each of us, becomes subject to a utility calculus – but one where, perversely, utility is defined as enhancing human control, for no intrinsic end.[151] We thus will be tempted to cease respecting ourselves and others as the unique disclosive beings that we in fact are.

7 Coda: Open Questions

This essay argues that there are two standing, core features of Heidegger's philosophy of science. (1) Heidegger critiques SCS, which he associates with physicalism and a progressive disclosure-avoidant tendency in modern science and metaphysics. And (2) he advances ACS; scientific research, he believes, is essentially founded on ontological disclosures and constantly open to the possibility of new ontological disclosures, which radically disrupt extant theories and practices but promise to open up access to previously unseen or poorly understood phenomena. Moreover, as I have argued, these two commitments about science are integrally bound up with Heidegger's broader concerns. They inform his analysis of the history of Western metaphysics, his discussions of the possibilities for (and hindrances to) human flourishing in modernity, and his efforts to reawaken our collective receptivity to ontological questioning and disclosure.

But many outstanding questions remain; I listed some of these in Section 1.1. Let me now close by adding just two more, which are especially prompted by the discussions in Sections 5 and 6.

---

[150] This phenomenon, let me suggest, is a basic feature of Heidegger's concept of modern nihilism. See NDHB 230–34, 239–42.

[151] We might reasonably ask to *whose* control things are subject. After all, modernity has hardly afforded the vast majority more control over their daily lives – see Marx (1978, p. 71, 1976, Chapters 10, 14, and 15). But this question is orthogonal to Heidegger's concept of technology. The aim of technology is not to expand the control of one class at the expense of another, even if, as is the case, technology results in greater class domination. Rather, the aim of technology is to ferry more things across the threshold from *entirely out of human control* to *under the possible control of some human*. For example, the invention of the airplane expanded the range of possible human control (over time, distance, and terrain) in the relevant Heideggerian sense, even though it failed to expand "human control" insofar as masses of people continue to lack the time, money, and access to infrastructure to fly.

First, does Heidegger find in quantum physics the potential for a transition beyond the technological assumptions that he finds so disastrous? He suggests as much in his well-known cryptic quotation of Hölderlin toward the end of QCT: "But where danger is, grows/The saving power also." Addressing this issue is all the more significant because quantum mechanics is not going away anytime soon, nor should it: after all, it has proven to be spectacularly empirically successful.

Second, in light of Heidegger's critique of the "industry" of science, what might scientific institutions look like if they were to be reformed along Heideggerian lines? This question is especially pressing given that Heidegger in fact had a vision for academic reform, and that he, at least for a time, saw the Nazi movement as a vehicle by which to enact it.[152] *Prima facie*, Heidegger's critique of SCS and support for ACS bear no connection to politics, let alone to Nazism. But this only underscores the necessity of a project that examines (1) the contents of his academic reform program, (2) why he saw the Nazi movement as a suitable vehicle by which to implement it, (3) how these concrete reforms do (or don't) relate to his critique of SCS and support for ACS, and (4) whether we can imagine an alternative suite of reforms consistent with Heidegger's critique of SCS and support for ACS but robustly consistent with liberal-democratic principles.

---

[152] See the texts collected in Part I of *HCCR* (esp. Heidegger's *Rektoratsrede*, *HCCR* 29–39). Thomson (2005) offers an excellent treatment of Heidegger's vision for academic reform focused especially on educational reform (see esp. Chapters 3–4).

References

Aquinas, Thomas. 1975. *Summa Contra Gentiles, Book One: God*. Trans. Anton C. Pegis. (Notre Dame, IN: University of Notre Dame Press).

Aristotle. 1984. *The Complete Works of Aristotle: The Revised Oxford Translation*. Ed. Jonathan Barnes. (Princeton, NJ: Princeton University Press). One-volume digital edition.

Augustine. 1995. *Against the Academicians and the Teacher*. Trans. Peter King. (Indianapolis, IN: Hackett).

Augustine. 2014. *Confessions: Books 1–8*. Trans. and ed. Carolyn J.-B. Hammond. (Cambridge, MA: Harvard University Press).

Augustine. 2016. *Confessions: Books 9–13*. Trans. and ed. Carolyn J.-B. Hammond. (Cambridge, MA: Harvard University Press).

Bacon, Francis. 2003. *The New Organon*. Ed. Lisa Jardine and Michael Silverthorne. (Cambridge: Cambridge University Press).

Beck, Adam. 2002. *Heidegger and Science: Nature, Objectivity and the Present-at-Hand*. (London: Middlesex University). PhD thesis. Awarded May 2002.

Beck, Adam. 2005. "Heidegger and Relativity Theory: Crisis, Authenticity, and Repetition." *Angelaki* 10(1). 163–79.

Blattner, William. 1995. "Decontextualization, Standardization, and Deweyan Science." *Man and World* 28(4). 321–39.

Blattner, William. 1999. *Heidegger's Temporal Idealism*. (Cambridge: Cambridge University Press).

Bokulich, Alisa. 2008. *Re-examining the Classical-Quantum Relation: Beyond Reductionism and Pluralism*. (Cambridge: Cambridge University Press).

Brandom, Robert. 1983. "Heidegger's Categories in *Being and Time*." *The Monist* 66(3). 387–409.

Brandom, Robert. 1997. "Dasein, the Being that Thematizes." *Epoché* 5. 1–38.

Buber, Martin. 1996. *I and Thou*. Trans. Walter Kaufmann. (New York: Touchstone).

Caputo, John D. 2012. "Heidegger's Philosophy of Science: The Two Essences of Science." In *Heidegger on Science*, pp. 261–79. Ed. Trish Glazebrook. (Albany: State University of New York Press).

Carman, Taylor. 2005. "Authenticity." In *A Companion to Heidegger*, pp. 285–96. Ed. Hubert L. Dreyfus and Mark A. Wrathall. (Malden, MA: Blackwell).

Carman, Taylor. 2007. "Heidegger on Correspondence and Correctness." *Graduate Faculty Philosophy Journal* 28. 103–16.

Carman, Taylor. 2019. "Quantum Theory as Technology." In *Heidegger on Technology*, pp. 299–313. Ed. Aaron James Wendland, Christopher Merwin, and Christos Hadjioannou. (New York: Routledge).

Carnap, Rudolph. 2011. *The Unity of Science*. Trans. Max Black. (New York: Routledge).

Carroll, Sean. 2019a. "Even Physicists Don't Understand Quantum Mechanics." *The New York Times*. September 7, 2019: www.nytimes.com/2019/09/07/opinion/sunday/quantum-physics.html.

Carroll, Sean. 2019b. *Something Deeply Hidden*. (New York: Dutton).

Carson, Cathryn. 2010a. "Science as Instrumental Reason: Heidegger, Habermas, Heisenberg." *Continental Philosophy Review* 42. 483–509.

Carson, Cathryn. 2010b. *Heisenberg in the Atomic Age: Science and the Public Sphere*. (Cambridge: Cambridge University Press).

Cassirer, Ernst. 2015. "Hermann Cohen and the Renewal of Kantian Philosophy." Trans. Lydia Patton. In *The Neo-Kantian Reader*, pp. 221–35. Ed. Sebastian Luft. (New York: Routledge).

Chevalley, Catherine. 1992. "Heidegger and the Physical Sciences." In *Martin Heidegger: Critical Assessments Volume IV: Reverberations*, pp. 342–64. Ed. Christopher Macann. (New York: Routledge).

Clark, Andy. 1999. *Being There: Putting Brain, Body, and World Together Again*. (Cambridge, MA: MIT Press).

Clarke, Leonard W. 1962. "Greek Astronomy and Its Debt to the Babylonians." *The British Journal for the History of Science* 1. 65–77.

Crease, Robert P. 2012. "Heidegger and the Empirical Turn in Continental Philosophy of Science." In *Heidegger on Science*, pp. 225–37. Ed. Trish Glazebrook. (Albany: State University of New York Press).

Crowell, Steven Galt. 1997. "Philosophy as a Vocation: Heidegger and University Reform in the Early Interwar Years." *History of Philosophy Quarterly* 14. 255–76.

Dahlstrom, Daniel O. 1995. "Heidegger's Concept of Temporality: Reflections on a Recent Criticism." *The Review of Metaphysics* 49. 95–115.

Dahlstrom, Daniel O. 2001. *Heidegger's Concept of Truth*. (Cambridge: Cambridge University Press).

Dahlstrom, Daniel O. 2005. "Heidegger and German Idealism." In *A Companion to Heidegger*, pp. 65–79. Ed. Hubert L. Dreyfus and Mark A. Wrathall. (Malden, MA: Blackwell).

Descartes, René. 1983. *Principles of Philosophy*. Trans. Valentine Rodger Miller and Reese P. Miller. (Dordrecht: D. Reidel).

Descartes, René. 1985. *The Philosophical Writings of Descartes*, Vol. 1. Trans. John Cottingham John Stoothoff and Dugald Murdoch. (Cambridge: Cambridge University Press).

Descartes, René. 1998. *Discourse on Method and Meditations on First Philosophy*. Trans. Donald A. Cress. (Indianapolis, IN: Hackett). 4th edition.

Dilthey, Wilhelm. 1977. *Descriptive Psychology and Historical Understanding*. Trans. Richard. M. Zaner and Kenneth L. Heiges. (The Hague: Martinus Nijhof).

Dreyfus, Hubert L. 1991. *Being-in-the-World: A Commentary on Heidegger's* Being and Time, *Division I*. (Cambridge, MA: MIT Press).

Dreyfus, Hubert L. 2004. "What Could Be More Intelligible than Everyday Intelligibility? Reinterpreting Division I of *Being and Time* in the Light of Division II." *Bulletin of Science, Technology & Society* 24. 265–74.

Dupré, John. 1983. "The Disunity of Science." *Mind* 92. 321–46.

Dupré, John. 1988. "Materialism, Physicalism, and Scientism." *Philosophical Topics* 16. 31–56.

Fedoroff, Nina V. 2012. "McClintock's Challenge in the 21st Century." *Proceedings of the National Academy of Sciences of the United States of America* 109. 20200–3.

Feyerabend, Paul. 1993. *Against Method*. (London: Verso). 3rd edition.

Glanzberg, Michael. 2021. "Truth." *The Stanford Encyclopedia of Philosophy*. Ed. Edward N. Zalta. Summer 2021 Edition: https://plato.stanford.edu/archives/sum2021/entries/truth/.

Glazebrook, Trish. 2000. *Heidegger's Philosophy of Science*. (New York: Fordham University Press).

Goldberg, Paul. 2021. "Two Refutations of the Vorhanden Reading of Heidegger's Philosophy of Science in *Being and Time*." *Heidegger Circle Proceedings* 55. 174–87.

Golob, Sacha. 2013. "Heidegger on Assertion, Method and Metaphysics." *European Journal of Philosophy* 23(4). 878–908.

Guignon, Charles B. 1983. *Heidegger and the Problem of Knowledge*. (Indianapolis, IN: Hackett).

Guignon, Charles B. 1993. "Authenticity, Moral Values, and Psychotherapy." In *The Cambridge Companion to Heidegger*, pp. 215–39. Ed. Charles B. Guignon. (Cambridge: Cambridge University Press).

Hanson, Norwood Russell. 1958. *Patterns of Discovery: An Inquiry into the Conceptual Foundations of Science*. (New York: Cambridge University Press).

Haugeland, John. 2013. *Dasein Disclosed: John Haugeland's Heidegger*. Ed. Joseph Rouse. (Cambridge, MA: Harvard University Press).

Heelan, Patrick A. 1995. "Heidegger's Longest Day: Twenty-Five Years Later." In *From Phenomenology to Thought, Errancy, and Desire: Essays in Honor of William J. Richardson, S.J.*, pp. 579–87. Ed. Babette E. Babich. (Dordrecht: Kluwer Academic).

Heidegger, Martin. See "Texts and Method of Citation" above.

Heisenberg, Werner. 1958a. "The Representation of Nature in Contemporary Physics." *Daedalus* 87. 95–108.

Heisenberg, Werner. 1958b. *Physics and Philosophy: The Revolution in Modern Science*. (London: George Allen & Unwin).

Hemming, Laurence Paul. 2013. *Heidegger and Marx: A Productive Dialogue over the Language of Humanism*. (Evanston, IL: Northwestern University Press).

Hempel, Carl G. 1965. *Aspects of Scientific Explanation and Other Essays in the Philosophy of Science*. (New York: The Free Press).

Hempel, Carl G. 1966. *Philosophy of Natural Science*. (Englewood Cliffs, NJ: Prentice-Hall).

Husserl, Edmund. 2001. *Logical Investigations*, Vol. 1. Trans. J. N. Findlay. Ed. Dermot Moran. (New York: Routledge).

Ihde, Don. 2010. *Heidegger's Technologies: Postphenomenological Perspectives*. (New York: Fordham University Press).

Käufer, Stephan. 2021. "Authenticity (*Eigentlichkeit*)." In *The Cambridge Heidegger Lexicon*, pp. 71–77. Ed. Mark A. Wrathall. (Cambridge: Cambridge University Press).

Keller, Evelyn Fox. 1983. *A Feeling for the Organism: The Life and Work of Barbara McClintock*. (San Francisco, CA: W.H. Freeman).

Kessel, Thomas. 2011. *Phänomenologie des Lebendigen: Heideggers Kritik an den Leitbegriffen der neuzeitlichen Biologie*. (Freiburg im Breisgau: Karl Alber).

Kisiel, Theodore. 1977. "Heidegger and the New Images of Science." *Research in Phenomenology* 7(1). 162–81.

Kisiel, Theodore and Thomas Sheehan (eds.). 2007. *Becoming Heidegger: On the Trail of His Early Occasional Writings, 1910–1927*. (Evanston, IL: Northwestern University Press).

Kitcher, Philip. 2011. *Science in a Democratic Society.* (Amherst, NY: Prometheus).

Kochan, Jeff. 2017. *Science as Social Existence: Heidegger and the Sociology of Scientific Knowledge*. (Cambridge: Open Book).

Kockelmans, Joseph J. 1985. *Heidegger and Science*. (Washington, DC: Center for Advanced Research in Phenomenology and University Press of America).

Kuhn, Thomas S. 2012. *The Structure of Scientific Revolutions*. (Chicago, IL: University of Chicago Press). 4th edition.

Lafont, Cristina. 2000. *Heidegger, Language, and World-Disclosure*. Trans. Graham Harman. (New York: Cambridge University Press).

Lakatos, Imre. 1970. "Falsification and the Methodology of Scientific Research Programmes." In *Criticism and the Growth of Knowledge*, pp. 91–196. Ed. Imre Lakatos and Alan Musgrave. (New York: Cambridge University Press).

Latour, Bruno and Steve Woolgar. 1979. *Laboratory Life: The Social Construction of Scientific Facts*. (Beverly Hills, CA: Sage).

Laughlin, R. B. and David Pines. 2000. "The Theory of Everything." *Proceedings of the National Academy of Sciences of the United States of America* 97(1). 28–31.

Longino, Helen E. 1990. *Science as Social Knowledge: Values and Objectivity in Scientific Research*. (Princeton, NJ: Princeton University Press).

Lotze, Rudolf Hermann. 2015. "The World of Ideas," from *Logic*. Trans. Bernard Bosanquet. In *The Neo- Kantian Reader*, pp. 82–92. Ed. Sebastian Luft. (New York: Routledge).

Luft, Sebastian (ed.). 2015. *The Neo-Kantian Reader*. (New York: Routledge).

Ma, Lin and Jaap van Brakel. 2014. "Heidegger's Thinking on the 'Same' of Science and Technology." *Continental Philosophy Review* 47. 19–43.

MacIntyre, Alasdair. 2007. *After Virtue: A Study in Moral Theory*. (Notre Dame, IN: The University of Notre Dame Press). 3rd edition.

Maimonides, Moses. 1910. *The Guide for the Perplexed*. Trans. Michael Friedländer. (New York: E.P. Dutton). 2nd edition.

Marx, Karl. 1976. *Capital: A Critique of Political Economy: Volume I*. Trans. Ben Fowkes. (London: Penguin).

Marx, Karl. 1978. "Estranged Labour." In *The Marx-Engels Reader*, pp. 70–81. Ed. Robert C. Tucker. (New York: Norton).

McManus, Denis. 2012. *Heidegger and the Measure of Truth*. (Oxford: Oxford University Press).

McManus, Denis. 2019. "On a Judgment of One's Own: Heideggerian Authenticity, Standpoints, and All Things Considered." *Mind* 128. 1181–204.

McNeill, William. 1999. *The Glance of the Eye: Heidegger, Aristotle, and the Ends of Theory*. (Albany: State University of New York Press).

Mitchell, Andrew. 2019. "The Question Concerning the Machine: Heidegger's Technology Notebooks in the 1940s-1950s." In *Heidegger on Technology*, pp. 115–32. Ed. Aaron James Wendland, Christopher Merwin, and Christos Hadjioannou. (New York: Routledge).

Natorp, Paul. 2015a. "Kant and the Marburg School." Trans. Frances Bottenberg. In *The Neo-Kantian Reader*, pp. 180–97. Ed. Sebastian Luft. (New York: Routledge).

Natorp, Paul. 2015b. "The Problem of a Logic of the Exact Sciences." Trans. Frances Bottenberg. In *The Neo-Kantian Reader*, pp. 198–213. Ed. Sebastian Luft. (New York: Routledge).

Nietzsche, Friedrich. 1969. *On the Genealogy of Morals and Ecce Homo*. Trans. Walter Kaufmann and R. J. Hollingdale. (New York: Vintage).

Nietzsche, Friedrich. 1974. *The Gay Science: With a Prelude in Rhymes and an Appendix of Songs*. Trans. Walter Kaufmann. (New York: Vintage).

Plato. 1997. *Plato: Complete Works*. Ed. John M. Cooper. (Indianapolis, IN: Hackett).

Pöggeler, Otto. 1993. "The Hermeneutics of the Technological World: The Heidegger – Heisenberg Dispute." Trans. Michael Kane and Kristin Pfefferkorn-Forbath. *International Journal of Philosophical Studies* 1. 21–48.

Popper, Karl. 2002. *The Logic of Scientific Discovery*. (New York: Routledge).

Quine, W. V. 1983. "Ontology and Ideology Revisited." *The Journal of Philosophy* 80. 499–502.

Quine, W. V. 2004. *Quintessence: Basic Readings from the Philosophy of W. V. Quine*. Ed. Roger F. Gibson, Jr. (Cambridge, MA: Harvard University Press).

Quine, W. V. 2013. *Word and Object*. (Cambridge, MA: MIT Press). New edition.

Reichenbach, Hans. 1938. *Experience and Prediction: An Analysis of the Foundations and the Structure of Knowledge*. (Chicago, IL: The University of Chicago Press).

Richardson, William J. 1968. "Heidegger's Critique of Science." *The New Scholasticism* 42. 511–36.

Rouse, Joseph. 1985a. "Science and the Theoretical 'Discovery' of the Present-at-Hand." In *Descriptions*, pp. 200–210. Ed. Don Ihde and Hugh J. Silverman. (Albany: State University of New York Press).

Rouse, Joseph. 1985b. "Heidegger's Later Philosophy of Science." *Southern Journal of Philosophy* 23(1). 75–92.

Rouse, Joseph. 1987. *Knowledge and Power: Toward a Political Philosophy of Science*. (Ithaca, NY: Cornell University Press).

Rouse, Joseph. 2005. "Heidegger's Philosophy of Science." In *A Companion to Heidegger*, pp. 173–89. Ed. Hubert L. Dreyfus and Mark A. Wrathall. (Malden, MA: Blackwell).

Sartre, Jean-Paul. 2007. *Existentialism Is a Humanism*. Trans. Carol Macomber. Ed. John Kulka. (New Haven, CT: Yale University Press).

Seigfried, Hans. 1978. "Heidegger's Longest Day: *Being and Time* and the Sciences." *Philosophy Today* 22. 319–31.

Seigfried, Hans. 1990. "Autonomy and Quantum Physics: Nietzsche, Heidegger, and Heisenberg." *Philosophy of Science* 57. 619–30.

Sheehan, Thomas. Unpublished Manuscript. "How Not to Translate Heidegger – 2: Dasein." Downloaded January 26, 2024. Available for download at: www .academia.edu/43179070/how_not_to_translate_heidegger_2_dasein_.

Singham, Mano. 2021. "When Lord Kelvin Nearly Killed Darwin's Theory." *Scientific American*, September 5, 2021: www.scientificamerican.com/art icle/when-lord-kelvin-nearly-killed-darwins-theory1/.

Sluga, Hans. 2005. "Heidegger's Nietzsche." In *A Companion to Heidegger*, pp. 102–20. Ed. Hubert L. Dreyfus and Mark A. Wrathall. (Malden, MA: Blackwell).

Smith, William H. 2007. "Why Tugendhat's Critique of Heidegger's Concept of Truth Remains a Critical Problem." *Inquiry* 50. 156–79.

Thomson, Iain. 2005. *Heidegger on Ontotheology: Technology and the Politics of Education.* (Cambridge: Cambridge University Press).

Thomson, Iain. 2011. *Heidegger, Art, and Postmodernity.* (Cambridge: Cambridge University Press).

Tugendhat, Ernst. 1994. "Heidegger's Idea of Truth." In *Hermeneutics and Truth*, pp. 83–97. Ed. Brice R. Wachterhauser. (Evanston, IL: Northwestern University Press).

van Fraassen, Bas C. 1980. *The Scientific Image.* (Oxford: Oxford University Press).

Watson, James R. 2012. "Beyond Ontic-Ontological Relations: Gelassenheit, Gegnet, and Niels Bohr's Program of Experimental Quantum Mechanics." In *Heidegger on Science*, pp. 47–65. Ed. Trish Glazebrook. (Albany: State University of New York Press).

Weber, Max. 2004. *The Vocation Lectures.* Trans. Rodney Livingstone. Ed. David Owen and Tracy B. Strong. (Indianapolis, IN: Hackett).

Wendland, Aaron James. 2019. "Heidegger vs. Kuhn: Does Science Think?" In *Heidegger on Technology*, pp. 282–98. Ed. Aaron James Wendland, Christopher Merwin, and Christos Hadjioannou. (New York: Routledge).

Withy, Katherine. 2015. *Heidegger on Being Uncanny.* (Cambridge, MA: Harvard University Press).

Wittgenstein, Ludwig. 1981. *Tractatus Logico-Philosophicus.* Trans. C. K. Ogden. (London: Routledge).

Wrathall, Mark A. 1999. "Heidegger and Truth as Correspondence." *International Journal of Philosophical Studies* 7. 69–88.

Wrathall, Mark A. 2011. *Heidegger and Unconcealment: Truth, Language, and History.* (New York: Cambridge University Press).

Acknowledgments

Thanks are due above all to Alex Campanelli for her advice and support and to my family and friends for their encouragement. Dan Dahlstrom, Iain Thomson, Alisa Bokulich, and Walter Hopp provided incisive feedback on earlier drafts of this research. I owe additional thanks to Dan and Filippo Casati for their work in editing this series, and to an anonymous reviewer, whose penetrating comments (and challenges) were immensely helpful. Dan Mendez and Andrew Butler helped me think through a number of thorny issues as they arose. My former colleagues, professors, and students at Boston University enriched my thinking immeasurably. William McNeill kindly provided an advance draft of his translation of GA27. Finally, let me thank Steven Hoeltzel, who many years ago introduced me to Heidegger's work and set an example of careful scholarship.

For Alex

Cambridge Elements ≡

The Philosophy of Martin Heidegger

About the Editors

Filippo Casati
Lehigh University

Filippo Casati is an Assistant Professor at Lehigh University. He has published an array of articles in such venues as *The British Journal for the History of Philosophy, Synthese, Logic et Analyse, Philosophia, Philosophy Compass* and *The European Journal of Philosophy.* He is the author of *Heidegger and the Contradiction of Being* (Routledge) and, with Daniel O. Dahlstrom, he edited *Heidegger on Logic* (Cambridge University Press).

Daniel O. Dahlstrom
Boston University

Daniel O. Dahlstrom, John R. Silber Professor of Philosophy at Boston University, has edited twenty volumes, translated Mendelssohn, Schiller, Hegel, Husserl, Heidegger, and Landmann-Kalischer, and authored *Heidegger's Concept of Truth* (2001), *The Heidegger Dictionary* (2013; second extensively expanded edition, 2023), *Identity, Authenticity, and Humility* (2017) and over 185 essays, principally on 18th-20th century German philosophy. With Filippo Casati, he edited *Heidegger on Logic* (Cambridge University Press).

About the Series

A continual source of inspiration and controversy, the work of Martin Heidegger challenges thinkers across traditions and has opened up previously unexplored dimensions of Western thinking. The Elements in this series critically examine the continuing impact and promise of a thinker who transformed early twentieth-century phenomenology, spawned existentialism, gave new life to hermeneutics, celebrated the truthfulness of art and poetry, uncovered the hidden meaning of language and being, warned of "forgetting" being, and exposed the ominously deep roots of the essence of modern technology in Western metaphysics. Concise and structured overviews of Heidegger's philosophy offer original and clarifying approaches to the major themes of Heidegger's work, with fresh and provocative perspectives on its significance for contemporary thinking and existence.

The Philosophy of Martin Heidegger

Elements in the Series

A full series listing is available at: www.cambridge.org/EPMH

Printed in the United States
by Baker & Taylor Publisher Services